The Hypnotic Wisdom of Presentation Mastery

Steve Ashman

Ashman Publishing

About the Author

Steve Ashman is a Certified Hypnotherapist, Stage Hypnotist and Master Practitioner of Neuro Linguistic Programming and works in practice in Leicestershire, England. As a therapist he specialises solely in weight management and Hypno-Band, hypnotic gastric band surgery.

In addition to therapy, Steve tours with his show 'The Hypnotic Wisdom of Weight Loss', sharing his experience in the field of weight management and how hypnosis can be used to fascinating effect to improve many aspects of your life.

Having worked in sales for over twenty five years, Steve offers in this book a unique approach to Presentation Mastery. You'll find out how to prepare exciting material, how to practice to perfection and perform so that your message and call to action has the greatest effect.

Steve is contactable through his web site at:

www.ashmanhypnosis.co.uk

Dedication

This work is dedicated to my wife, Marion Ashman
for her love and support, to my friends and
colleagues who work tirelessly in this industry and all
of my clients that have benefited from hypnosis over
the years.

Copyright

Contents

Let's cut to the chase

If you have purchased this book because your need is to do an urgent presentation tomorrow, then go straight to Section 2 – Practice.

If you have purchased this book because you want to learn the art of Presentation Mastery, then read on.

Introduction

Most people would rather die than give a presentation! How many times have you heard that saying? Standing up and talking to people can be extremely stressful. As an audience member you can instantly tell the difference between someone that is nervous and those that have a natural and fearless ability to entertain, whilst managing to get their message across.

Well I'm here to tell you, we all have the resources inside of ourselves to be outstanding. This book explores the traits and techniques of the World's greatest orators. The Hypnotic Wisdom of Presentation Mastery will give you all the skills you need to prepare, practice and perform a presentation, whether it's a 1-on-1 conversation with a colleague to negotiate on ideas, to wow family and friends as a best man or bridegroom, or even to command attention with an on-stage performance. This book will take you through each of the important steps that you need to be a success.

So what has public speaking and presentation training got to do with hypnosis?

Hypnosis encompasses a number of specific competences that closely relate to presentations and is a performance art form in itself. The hypnotist's art relies on the mastery of communication to affect behavioural change (hypnotherapy) and flamboyant showmanship to entertain an audience (stage hypnosis). The skills and techniques offered in this book allow you to benefit from over twenty five years of presentation experience. As a public speaker, stage hypnotist, hypnotherapist and sales trainer, I am going to peel back the secrets, build your confidence and give you an effective tool box to make you a master presenter.

What is a presentation?
The definition of a presentation is an important one. People from all walks of life are required to impart their knowledge to others at some point in their career and even those who aspire to stardom through performance need to project their speciality in a convincing way. This topic has a wide spectrum, here are just some of presentation possibilities:

- A conversation with a friend to suggest a foreign holiday and get them to agree!
- Negotiating with your team for a change in working practices
- A sales presentation to a customer

- An Agile or Prince2 project meeting
- A sports coach motivating a team prior to a game
- Your introduction to the judges on Britain's got talent
- A manager motivating office staff
- A manager conducting a sales meeting via Skype
- The reading of a eulogy
- A doctor giving bad news to a patient
- A bingo caller
- A comedian preparing for a show
- A stage hypnotist
- A politician making an acceptance speech
- Giving a case study demonstration on stage
- A best man/bridegroom addressing family and friends
- A Burn's night supper speaker
- A 1 minute presentation at a business breakfast meeting
- A coach tour presenter speaking over the bus public address system
- A charity fund raiser
- An after dinner speaker
- A thank you speech at an awards party
- Selling vegetables on a market stall

This list is by no means exhaustive. A presentation is simply a technique to impart information to others. The information can be anything, it is your objective that is important. If you are a doctor dealing with a terminally ill patient your objective in the communication will be entirely different to a manager in a sales office trying to motivate people, but the preparation is exactly the same.

The presentation itself will be a subjective experience for all those involved. By the end of this book, as a professional presenter, you will have the skills to prepare unrivalled content, deliver a captivating performance and the ability to critique and review your efforts to ensure that your objectives are met.

What are the traits of great presenter?
Great presenters captivate their audiences. When you see a great presenter in action, your mind remains focussed and motivated throughout. Your attention allows you to hang on every word. They use words and pictures that fuel your imagination. No matter how large or trivial the message is, a great presenter will always find ways to stimulate your unconscious thinking to accept the idea.

A great presenter has clearly defined traits.

1. The ability to transport the audience through a range of emotional states appropriate to the objective of the presentation.
2. The adeptness to create new behaviours in the audience.

3. The ability to act as a natural leader.
4. They remain cool, calm and collected throughout.
5. The flexibility to adapt to the needs and reactions of the audiences.
6. A desire to be the best, a specialist or trusted advisor.
7. They put the needs of the audience first.

Emotional states

A truly memorable presentation will trigger a range of emotions inside an individual. After all, emotion is the driving force of change. When you set out to make a sizeable purchase for your home, say furniture or a home cinema system, can you remember the range of emotions that made you want to buy?

Let's say for example, your partner and you have decided to buy a new flat screen TV. You've read the 'Which' reports and in your mind the most appropriate piece of equipment for you is the XXXX model. You enter the department store and the manager comes over to speak to you (gives you a presentation).

The manager asks questions and you explain your thoughts and your intention to buy. In your eyes, this is a simple transaction. You know what you want. You are looking forward to the new purchase (an emotion) and have indicated your intention to buy (a buying signal).

The manager listens intently and then empathises (tells a true story).

"I can see why you would want the XXXX model, it is an exceptionally good piece of equipment and we have sold hundreds of these over the last few months. (It's true, you read it in the 'Which' magazine) We had a customer in here just this week with the same intention. He had an almost identical requirement. My colleague John (my friend John technique – I will share this with you later) served him, but not before showing the customer something new. (The emotional state of curiosity is being introduced) As with all equipment of this nature, new models always offer so much more for the same price..."

You can imagine the situation can't you? The manager appears to be doing his job. He is not trying to take more money from you or sell you something that you don't want. He is broadening your horizons by creating the most powerful emotional state of all, curiosity. He is opening a door you hadn't considered. Of course, the objectives of the manager will dictate which pieces of equipment to sell the public and as long as the recommendation takes in the best interests of the customer we have a win-win situation.

Emotions are exceptionally powerful. We have established that the emotional state of curiosity can be useful to build the buying potential of a customer in the sale. In the same way, a cinema manager may entice a new audience by saying.

"...and you'll never believe what film we are showing next month (long pause for dramatic effect).....well if you come into reception next Monday I will tell you."

But, what about a charity collector collating funds for cancer research, what emotional states would they need to employ?

A professional charity fund raiser may choose to use sadness or reflection in their speech as a reminder to us all that, it could happen to us. But beware, to leave your audience in negatively emotional states for too long may be detrimental to achieving their goal of fund raising. They may find the presentation journey begins with happiness (to get the audience interested), changing to sadness and loss (to reflect the heartache that the condition or problem causes) and completes with enthusiasm (to show that personal donations are giving new hope).

By moving seamlessly between emotions the presenter turns a difficult subject into a captivating and thought provoking masterpiece.

Developing behaviours
The presentation you set out to give will have many objectives. You may need to sell an item or train a group of people on your product or even thank a group of friends for their kind wedding gifts.   It is important that

you set an objective, this will be covered in detail in a later chapter.

In the majority of presentations though you will want to create new behaviours in your invited guests. These behaviours are intrinsic to the success of your objectives. You will want each person in attendance to:

- Feel great
- Act on the information you give them
- Feel empowered and not hopeless
- Ask lots of questions
- Feel an urge to get involved.

Everyone wants to feel good. Nothing is worse in a training session than being told you are not as good as you should be. It may be a useful part of the course to include pressure or criticism, but you must ensure that every delegate leaves feeling great or you damage your chances of motivating that person in the future. Even if you only see them once, you want every person in the audience to leave the presentation with a good word for you, even if they don't like your product or political views or ideas on what charity giving really means.

There is no point in taking time out to prepare for a presentation, getting up and doing a great job if the audience does not act on your information. Be clear!

- Do we want them to buy?
- Do we want them to sign a petition?

- Do we want them to sign a feedback form to say our training was excellent?
- Do we want our family and friends to feel appreciated and spread a good word about your intentions?

By making your audience feel empowered, you give them the opportunity to go out and continue your hard work. Feeling empowered is an emotional state that has the ability to continue long after your presentation has ended. The opposite emotion of hopelessness has the effect of stalling all positive intention in a person. By flicking that switch to positive you are seen as the motivator that everyone wants to be with.

The topic of questions in a presentation is covered in more detail later in this book. We fear that an awkward question will destroy our hard work, but this is rarely the truth. By ensuring clarity in your performance, the questions you receive from the audience will only strengthen your message. Questions show that the audience are really interested in the topic that you have presented.

A natural leader

When you stand in front of an audience and give a presentation they expect you to be the expert, the specialist, the trusted advisor or why would you be there? The audience wants you to give them value for the time they give up. In essence, they are willing you to do well.

So many brilliant people fall at the first hurdle by apologising for not having all the detail or not being prepared or telling the world that this is their first time as a presenter. When you are negative the audience picks up on those signals immediately and you are setting yourself up to fail. When you are positive and enthusiastic your wave of friendliness masks any areas where you think the presentation could have gone better or have said the wrong thing. When you stand up your body language, demeanour and vocal tone should set a commanding example. You turn into the alpha male/female in the room, the leader that has all the skills and makes all the decisions. Your presentation leaves no one in doubt that you are the boss.

To help you, let's look at the make-up of a natural leader:

- Believes 100% in their topic, product, service, company, friendship – whatever it is that they are talking about. This is one of the benefits of television. If you watch a documentary or informative programme made by someone who is enthusiastic, you can't help to be drawn into the content even if the subject isn't one you would normally subscribe to.
- Body positive – Stand up straight when you talk. Put your shoulders back and command the stage. A natural leader has presence and commitment.

When you are properly prepared you won't need to feel embarrassed or self-conscious.

- Eye contact – look your audience in the eye. This simple gestures tells them you are honest and that you truly believe what you are saying. Good eye contact will make your audience believe you are specialist in your field.
- Vocal tonality, speed and volume – nothing affects emotion more than the sound of the spoken voice. Your voice is the most versatile tool in your arsenal. Always speak clearly because clarity allows a positive result to form without misunderstanding. As you'll learn in later chapters, great presenters use stories to get their message across, who would want a monotone narrative.
- Silence - A natural leader will use the voice to emphasise information in the presentation. Silence builds tension, tension builds curiosity. When you create a situation where the audience hangs on every word……….anything can happen.
- Control – Leaders in any walk of life are in control. They lead the way for others to follow. They never falter on giving the right message, again and again with congruency. You know your subject, you are a specialist and the advice you give can be trusted. Don't generalise.

Motivation

- Why do you <u>want</u> to do this speech?
- Why do you <u>have</u> to do this speech?

You are reading this book for a reason. Maybe, you have always wanted to be an after dinner speaker or your child's wedding is coming up and you want to make a good impression or through promotion your career demands you step up and motivate your team. Either way the route to success is the same. With a decisive deadline and a positive objective in your sights, you can become a presentation master.

By the time you finish this book you will have all the skills to ensure you are fully motivated for the task ahead. Just by being prepared and practiced, you will banish all other negative thoughts and have the tools and resources to focus on the job in hand.

Fear of failure

I said at the start of this chapter that some people would rather die than give a presentation. What is it that creates such an irrational fear? Something triggers inside the mind that creates the fear, in the same way that we develop a fear of spiders or flying or the colour red. Yet, in other people's eyes irrational fear is meaningless and they cannot understand why a person would be so affected.

You may have heard the phrase, all behaviour (including fear) is a learned response. We are only born with two behaviour patterns, the fear of falling backwards and the fear of loud bangs. Every other fear has been created in the years between now and when we were born.

Take presentation fear. Why do we worry? Is it that we think the audience won't like us. Or is it that you don't feel worthy or capable? Or is it that people in the audience will have more knowledge than you and doubt your intentions?

Without the knowledge in this book you will continue to feel this stress. No matter how many times you sit down to prepare, the anxiety will build. It may be true that the words you have written on paper read well, in fact as you read the words you may even have a picture of the event in your mind. Often, a few days before the presentation your sleeping pattern will change. Your unconscious mind will take over and try to find reason in what you are doing. The unconscious mind will question every aspect of what you are going to say and how you are going to act. Comments from friends, family and colleagues will all have an effect on your positivity and sleep.

Set out to enjoy this process. From the moment you decide that the presentation will take place, in your mind turn the presentation into an actual event. Follow the instructions in this book closely and be prepared for the accolade that master presenters create.

Massive success begins with visualisation

Put all thoughts of fear to one side. Close your eyes and visualise the presentation with a positive outcome. This is an important hypnotic principle. See the presentation and the goal in your mind's eye in great detail. Close your eyes and...

1. See the audience arrive. Allow yourself to mingle with them as they take their seats. Take notice of how they are feeling. Warm, in good spirits, chatty, bright eyed and looking forward to the event.
2. Imagine what it would be like to sit in the audience and see yourself walking onto the stage. How do you look? Smart, shoulders back, a smile on your face, in control and commanding attention.
3. Listen to your greeting and first words. Can everyone in the audience hear clearly? Take a look at the back of the room is everybody engaged with you before you proceed. Wave to the ones that are still talking, clap your hands and let the room know in a loud voice this presentation is going to be great!
4. See yourself moving around the stage as you speak, keeping your eye contact moving, making everyone feel included. Your body language is open and welcoming.
5. Look for the changes in emotion in your presentation and the audience's reaction. When

you lower your tone are they still engaged? Emphasise a point with silence. Nod your head and make sure everyone has taken that piece of information in, before you talk again.

6. Go for the big finish. Finish on a high, or a call to action. Begin a round of applause yourself and see what happens. Feel the pride inside of yourself for a job well done.

Visualisation is a technique used by athletes and sports men and women to mentally prepare for the goal ahead. It may not be a verbal presentation they are about to give, although they do have a clearly defined objective to win. Visualisation means that they mentally rehearse every aspect of their performance before taking the stage. I'm sure this visualisation process can be broken down for your individual needs. Give it a go, you'll be surprised by the results. Follow these steps:

1. Map out the order of the presentation.
2. Break it down into small segments you can remember when you have your eyes closed.
3. Practice each segment and get it right before moving on to the next. Each picture you create in your mind should be in full colour, with sound. You may slow down the film so that you can focus in on the detail.
4. Once is never enough. Make visualisation a habit.
5. Practice does make perfect. Only practice over and over, when you know you have the pictures and sounds, the best they can be.

In the next chapter we begin to break down the process so that the visualisation comes true.

Prepare, Practice, Perform

Prepare - See what I did there? Three words that begin with P. Oh my word is that a presentation technique, shush - don't tell anyone, we'll cover that technique shortly. The three 'P's, obvious isn't it. First of all we are going to prepare the content of our presentation. Of course, you might think that all great presenters ad lib fantastic material.

Think back to Winston Churchill in World War 2. He was one of the greatest orators that this country had ever seen.

"Never in the field of human conflict has so much been owed to so few..."

I wasn't even born when this speech took place, but that line is one of the most memorable of all time. What about four little words that changed the face of this earth forever.

"I have a dream." - Martin Luther King

Great presenters do not ad lib. They perform great material. A great presenter enthrals, entices and makes the audience believe in the magic of their presentation. The way the words are delivered is more to do with mannerism, emotion and body language than it is to do with the actual words.

Do you think Martin Luther King was saying he wished the world would be a better place or do you think the story he had in his head was a lot more powerful. His words would take the listener on a journey starting with the here and now, a place of lethargy and despair for many Americans. The speech would move on through the emotion of curiosity 'this is what the world could be', the tension being created by the silence while on lookers use their own subconscious minds to build that picture. By the time Martin Luther King delivered the final words of the speech the audience was moving with him. A powerful crescendo of words building an emotional high. By the end of the speech, do you think the audience were completely sold on his ideas?

When you write your material and perform it, deliver each piece of information with thoughtfulness. Create dynamic tension using silence and the occasional pause. Make the audience feel like this is the first moment that you are imparting this information on them. Make them feel special.

The script is an important factor in any great presentation, but it can be the greatest enemy at the same time. Heed my warning. A written script is no substitute for practising out loud. Never hold a full script in your hands and read it! (More on this later)

Practice – The mind is a wonderful place to try out new ideas. You can enter a trance and build the entire scenario in your mind, visualisation is a brilliant habit to get into. But, when it comes to practice there is one main rule.

Do it

out

loud!

Humming away to yourself in the corner of a room is not sufficient practice. Make sure you practice out loud. The spoken word is picked up by your ears and processed by your mind. You get the chance to interpret the words and meaning first hand. The words always sound different when said, out loud.

When you write a book in a long hand style, it may read well. That's what it's supposed to, it's a piece of literary work or instruction. Using the same words on stage can be disastrous. When you say the same words out loud, sentences can often sound too full.   If they sound too full the message will be lost on the audience. Less is more. In the section, practice, we'll discuss how to rehearse, how long to rehearse and how to refine the material so that your message has the greatest impact.

Perform – Some of you may be thinking, I am not a performer. I can't jump around on the stage. I don't want to make a fool of myself. I want to get the job done and get off the stage as soon as possible.

I agree. You do not want to look foolish. You want to look and act like the specialist, the trusted advisor, the professional. There are many techniques you can use to improve how you are perceived.   Now it's time to get started.

Section 1 - Prepare

It's time to get down to the detail and be specific, in fact it's time to <u>SMILE</u>. Did I do it again? Did I just follow on from three 'P's with an acronym – SMILE. Like I said they are techniques, a way of getting your audience to remember the content of your presentation.

SMILE is an acronym of:

- Set objectives
- Method
- Imagination
- Less is more
- Evaluate

SMILE - Set objectives

As a lorry driver you need to know exactly where you are going at the start of the journey or you may never know when to stop delivering and time may become an issue. In the same way, clear objectives are needed in every type of presentation. A start, the main detail and a strong ending should be applied to every situation. Without these things clearly defined, preparation becomes impossible.

- What is the main purpose of the presentation?
- Why are you there?
- Why are you in the driving seat?

As an example, let's say I have been asked to give a talk about hypnosis to a local sports club. I need to ask a few more questions before I accept the invitation. On the face of it, it may look like another great opportunity to do what I love, but you will need to meet the requirements of the organiser within your remit. I may ask:

- How old are the audience?
- How long do you need me to talk?
- Are there any specific themes you need me to include/exclude?
- What lasting thought would you like me to leave them with?
- Is this part of a larger presentation, if it is, what are the other topics?
- What equipment do I need to bring with me?

In my case, the content of the show will differ depending on age and the laws associated with it. From my repertoire of material, I can choose various examples of work depending on the time we have available. If it's a sports club I would expect the manager to want a positive message, promoting a healthy lifestyle and high motivation for training. I can easily add this if asked. If I'm on stage alongside other speakers I work my material into the comments of previous speakers on the night, this makes the whole event look cohesive. I tend to always use my own lights and public address system as it can be relied on to work without a hitch, but larger venues may offer better alternatives that I may wish to use.

Each situation will be different. Let's say that you want to sell an idea to your bosses at work. You may introduce your idea to a line manager by saying,

"I have a great idea for saving money on the manufacturing production line. Do you think I could book 30 minutes with you on Friday to discuss the detail?"

Your question alone will have created sufficient curiosity to warrant a positive response.

In this type of question, what are the possible answers?

- No, I'm too busy
- Tell me now, I'm curious
- Yes, let's make it 11am
- Yes, but keep it short, I'll give you 10 minutes to see if it's a viable proposition

Managers should love employees that ask them questions like that. Whatever you do, don't spill the beans before the formal presentation. Think about it. You aren't prepared, so it may not go as well as can expected. Your manager may be too busy and make a snap decision. This is not what you are looking for.

In this scenario, we have our timescale. We have the length of the presentation, when it is scheduled for so that we can prepare and who we are presenting to. Of course, you should confirm the meeting in diaries and by email to make sure it happens and include as many of the important people as possible.

Your goal is to convince your line manager that you are credible, that you have an idea that will save the company money and to provide enough information so that your idea is taken up.

Now let's take the example of the best man or bridegroom at a wedding. What would be their objectives? Weddings differ around the world these days. There are traditional white weddings with all of the pomp and circumstance and custom afforded to each region. These will include stringent guidelines you need to be aware of. Others may be more flexible at the bequest of the wedding party, all you need to know is when is it going to happen and what are the facilities like.

Having been a best man on a number of occasions in my life I can tell you that asking these simple questions early on in the arrangements can save you a lot of time and heartache. Some modern wedding arrangements may require the need of a public address system and microphone, again without prior use, the sound of your own voice being fed back to you can often shatter the hard work taken in rehearsals.   By asking a few simple questions, you can be prepared for almost every eventuality.

What's in it for them?

The audience are the most important part of this performance. Not you. Not your self-esteem. As an audience we give up our time to listen. We pray that the presentation is going to be good, it's as if we will the performer to do well. No one wants to see an ill prepared speaker that waffles for hours. We want to leave the performance with information that we can use or in the example of the wedding speaker, a competent few words that cement the appreciation of the family and your friendship.

When you are preparing and write your first words on the paper. Test your material with:

So Wot!

Let's look at a sales person standing in the shopping precinct selling vehicle breakdown insurance (a presentation). Can you use the So Wot! Statement at the end of these pieces of information.

- "The DRB Association is the largest vehicle recovery company in the nation."
- "Our mechanics will be on site as quickly as possible."
- "No one does vehicle recovery like we do."

If these approaches are used to hook new customers you wouldn't be surprised if trade were a little slow. In each of these examples what impact does the information have on the intended audience, it may be mildly relevant, but offers absolutely no benefit to the listener. Let's try again.

- "The DRB Association is the largest vehicle recovery company in the nation, which means that when you are making that important journey to the airport, ferrying your grandchildren to school and visiting family anywhere in the country, you can be sure that we have mechanics nearby to get you back on the road quickly."
- "Our mechanics will be on site as quickly as possible, giving you piece of mind that you will never be stuck on the motorway, we'll have you back on your journey without delay."
- "No one does vehicle recovery like we do. Being the biggest, strongest financially and proven experts, ensures that you get the most out of your investment."

In fairness, this is a technique that was taught to me on my first day of sales training and it's worked successfully for all these years.   Often when we give a presentation we speak outwardly to an audience and rarely hear the impact of our words. This is another important concept of hypnosis, the effect your words have on the people you are presenting to. There are two perceptual positions you need to consider. Position 1 is the presenter (how you say the words) and position 2 are the people listening (how those words are perceived). Imagine you are the customer, is this what you want to hear? Say to yourself:

"What's in it for me?"

The audience will only stay engaged if there is something in the presentation for them.

The technique is called FAB's or Features, Advantages and Benefits. A feature is simply that. Something you, the product or service will do. An advantage tells the listener that the feature will actually give them something in return for its purchase. For instance, a light bulb (feature), will cast light into a room (advantage).

Neither the feature nor the advantage really give a compelling reason to buy now. However, if you were to say:

"This light bulb (feature), casts light into a room (advantage), which means that your elderly mother will no longer have to strain her eyes (benefit) to read the magazine."

The construction of this sentence is compelling. As long as the statement is true that their elderly mother does like to read, which son in the world wouldn't buy the light bulb, as long as it was within financial reach.

The same technique can be used in a wedding speech. You could say:

"Toby (the bridegroom) is a good friend of mine, a trustworthy and thoughtful person."

It's a nice thing to say, but it could be more meaningful. Try:

"Toby is a good friend of mine, a trustworthy and thoughtful person, all characteristics that I believe will make him the ideal husband."

An elaboration that close relatives will greatly appreciate.

What's in it for them?

Sit yourself in the audience and prepare the content from their point of view.

Know your subject
There's a good chance that you've been asked to speak at this event because you are the specialist in your field. You know the ins and outs of the industry or subject and this is your opportunity to teach others.

I said in the last section, know your audience. You will need to pitch at their level. If you are an expert rock climber and the audience is a room full of retirees at a lunch club you may find it more appealing to focus on the achievements, geography and challenges of your climbs. If the audience is a rock climbing club, then that's a whole different matter. Add the detail that matters. The type of equipment, the routes up the mountain, where it went wrong and where you triumphed, could all be woven into the story.

I said earlier, the audience is willing you to do well. They will know you are the specialist. You've probably been billed as the world renowned specialist in XXXX and they've turned up to see you. Even if the billing wasn't that grand, the way you walk on the stage and talk about the subject with congruency is going to sell you as a professional. Congruency means that what you are saying matches your body language and your inner intention. The audience has to believe you. Trust comes from a perfect match of congruency.

If you know your subject, the audience will be willing to let you off with mistakes, because what you are saying comes from a trustworthy source and the passion you have for the subject. You will also find that it is easy for you to take questions on the subject, responding with truthful answers that are highly informative.

Remember though, being good at your subject is not enough. The technique in this book will transform your message into something really special. Professional presenters are able to competently hold an audience even if they don't know the subject, in your particular case as a specialist this will create additional magic.

You never get a second chance to make a first impression

It is human nature to initially judge a situation whilst you gather further information. You may walk into a bar and with wide peripheral vision quickly come to a conclusion about the people that are dotted around the room. Within seconds you'll get a feeling if the atmosphere in the room is friendly or if the people and their behaviour appeal to your prerequisite needs.

This is a natural instinct. So often, we build an opinion about celebrities from snippets of news which may or may not be proven or accurate, the same is true in your presentation. As you walk onto the stage, the audience will be assessing the way you walk and act from the moment they see you. Let's think about the type of audience for a moment. The people in the audience will either be known to you, friends, family or colleagues or unknown to you.

People that know you have a preconceived idea of how you are going to act, how you are going to speak and will have a good idea of the quality of what is about to come. That was before you started to read The Hypnotic Wisdom of Presentation Mastery and decided to change your approach. In some ways, this is the harder audience. Your friends will have known you all your life and it is difficult for them to see you in a different light.

Stay focussed and act professional. Dress appropriately for the occasion, showing respect for the attendees. It may not be a wise move to wear jeans and a hoody top at a wedding if you want to build the right impression, unless of course, that's the theme for the day. From the very second people see you, their peripheral vision will take in everything about you. For me, polishing my shoes and adorning a business suit was a must.

The secret of a great presentation is that you achieve a confidence level in the room during the entire performance. If the audience is confident in your abilities they will take on board every word that you say. Like I've said before, if the audience don't know you, they will be wanting you to do well. Follow the rules in this book and wow that audience.

How do people learn?
If the purpose of your presentation is to inform, then be aware that we all learn in different ways. The majority of the population learn from seeing things (visual orientation), with a smaller percentage taking information on board by sound (auditory) and a smaller percentage with their feelings (kinaesthetic). We are also influenced by smell and taste in certain situations (olfactory/gustatory). The last two methods of learning will prove invaluable if you are suppliers of food and beverages. You can bring all of these five methods into action at any time to enrich the quality of the performance.

The de-facto standard in business presentations is the use of Microsoft PowerPoint. Used correctly PowerPoint is a powerful medium that can help develop an idea in the minds of the delegates. However, as I will explain later PowerPoint can be abused often to the extent that you turn off the ability of the delegate to learn, this known as 'Death by PowerPoint'.

A presentation is the use of your imagination. Set yourself free. Let your ideas take shape before you dismiss their possibilities. The most memorable presentation I remember, almost word for word was not long and did not use PowerPoint to sell its qualities.

Let me set the scene for you. The seminar was a mixture of speakers discussing the latest technologies in computer hardware and software and was directed at business owners. First of all we'd listened intently to the Managing Director of the business group discussing growth scenarios and how this day would help everyone expand their profitability. Followed by a number of speakers establishing their name as market leading suppliers, then the mood changed.

Over the public address system music was played. Sombre, funeral music which changed the atmosphere, creating an air of awkwardness. My colleague took the floor wearing a black shirt with his tie having been replaced by a wide collar band. If I'm not mistaken cut from a white washing up bottle to make him look like a vicar. The music continued to play, although lower in volume while he spoke.

"Dearly beloved, we are gathered here today to mourn the loss of data. Data was a valuable friend...."

I will remember that first line of the speech forever, it really grabbed everyone's attention, a showstopper. You could have heard a pin drop whilst the audience listened.

Now the whimsical discussion of data security was now taking place without the presenter mentioning the real issues. Over the next three or four minutes the angelic words discussed how losing data in a business is disastrous. When it happens the analogy of death is very similar indeed, often businesses cannot survive.

At the end of the presentation the music stopped and with ultimate timing he applied pressure and urgency to the situation with silence, before pulling a slim hard drive from his jacket pocket. He waved it frantically.

"These things are only £129, how can you not afford to buy one today?"

In fairness, few transactions were ever made at these events, but on that date a number of orders were taken immediately.

People learn in an up time trance. You cannot teach your children anything if they are in a bad mood, for instance. Make them happy, grab their attention, get them to really enjoy the subject and the learning will begin. There are lots of ways to grab attention, to let the learning begin. Here are just a few ideas.

- Sellotape an envelope to the bottom of the chair which the audience have to hunt for, the options are endless. In the envelope have:
  - An answer to a question with a prize ticket.
  - Some personal information about one of the staff members that they need to discover before the end of the day.
  - A question. This is brilliant. In each of the envelopes put a question that you would want the audience to ask although they may be too scared to. Then point at a chair and say: "Can I have your question please?" They pull out the envelope and the speaker says 'great question madam, I wish I had thought of that!', whilst smiling vivaciously. Then go on to give a highly accurate and professional explanation.
- The smell of baking bread
  - If you are about to show a family around a show home, play with their imagination:
  - Paint a picture of where the family will have Christmas dinner.
  - How the views over the countryside will create a conducive atmosphere for any writer.
  - How the drive will easily accommodate the vehicles of the growing family.

- These ideas will develop as you ask more questions of the potential buyer's needs.
- A costume or prop
  - Change the norm. A stuffy business suit won't always entice attention. Tie the theme of the costume into your story.
- Audience participation
  - I'm sure you can appreciate sitting still and listening is hard work. Especially if the presentation is part of an all-day event and your allocated time is the graveyard slot just after lunch.
  - I recently saw a speaker who hosted an all-day sales celebration. He motivated the audience to move around after lunch. In the morning he'd spoken about his life in the army as a paratrooper and how his life had changed. After lunch he donned physical education fatigues and made the room exercise as if in the army. The energy cleared away any remaining cobwebs allowing another bout of learning.

The human psychology of presentation

A presentation should be treated as a contiguous journey of imparted knowledge and entertainment. Without appropriate rehearsal this process can easily sound as if the presenter is reading from a faceless script. Television presenters have to master the art of reading the autocue whilst making the information sound as if they are having a conversation with the camera. I must emphasise, I am not asking you to go out and buy an autocue. With The Hypnotic Wisdom of Presentation Mastery your technique of delivery will develop naturally.

Presentations need a start, a middle and an end. At the beginning you start with an upbeat attitude, state your objectives and inform the audience how long you are going to talk for. There is nothing worse than an audience continually looking at their watches wondering when the next coffee break will come. If this happens you have already lost them.

If you inform them that your presentation is going to take the next 30 minutes and they will learn the three most important techniques in needlework, as long as your audience is interested in the subject they will respond well, as long as you stick to your promises. At some point in the process delegates will get lost in their own internal thoughts, they go inside so to speak and see your information in their own reality. This is good, we want them to visualise solutions. What we don't want them to do is wander off and think of something completely different. An audience will always come back on line strongly with full attention, shortly before the end of the presentation.

Time is valuable and your nemesis. If you finish too quickly the organisers have to make up the additional time and you may lose the attention of some of the audience. If you overrun, the audience lose out on additional coffee time and your hard work closing successfully is lost. Respect time at all times. A great presenter practices their material until the time aspect is mastered.

The middle part of the presentation is where you put the majority of the detail. In a thirty minute slot, you may need five minutes for the start and five minutes for the end leaving twenty minutes for the middle section. Twenty minutes sounds like a lot of time doesn't it? It isn't. When you prepare properly, it is a whirlwind in time. When it comes to the human brain, if you deliver any more than three items of information it will be lost. So don't cram too much in to the time. The topic of 'The less is more' is covered in more detail in a moment.

Then the end. At the end of the presentation you need to cement the core values of the message. Re-iterate what is important and state your call to action, so that something happens. Make it memorable. Tell the audience where they can get more information and how to follow up with you, if this is your objective.

As people, we like to know where we stand. If this is your first attempt at public speaking hang around afterwards and gleam feedback from the audience or bask in the adulation that you will surely deserve.

This leaves the middle part of the presentation. Essentially, what to say. Aim to add emotional value into the journey and ensure smooth transitions between each topic. What emotional states or behaviours do you really want the audience to experience?

Curiosity is something I want all of my delegates to feel at the start of a presentation. Curiosity is a characteristic that makes you want to carry on listening. Take a shop window display of the latest high street fashions, does it make you want to enter the store to find out more? It does. It builds a picture of possibility and leaves room for more questions, which of course, you have to enter the shop to ask.

As an example, you may be talking to a group of leading industrialists about the benefits of achieving new green emissions guidelines. You might start the detail section of your presentation with:

"You might be wondering how a company of this size can achieve all of these requirements and remain profitable and sustainable. Well, I'm here to show you exactly how we did this. Is this something you'd like to see?"

Wait for the answer. Look for the nods around the room and the interest. A pause at this moment is valuable.

Another way to generate curiosity is to say:

"In a moment I'm going to tell you about the time we broke the rules and got away with it, but first let me…." Don't give the important information away first. Make the audience work. Enticing them with information will help them pay attention until the right time.

In the main section of the presentation you may choose to change the mood using positive or negative emotions. If you set out to keep your entire thirty minute presentation on a high you will lose some of the audience along the way. You can make an audience excited, but the high will only last a few minutes at best, so mix up your emotional trail.

Positive emotions may include, feeling excited, empowered, happiness, laughter, feeling great, etc.

Negative ones may include sadness, fear, loss, anger, hopelessness, etc.

In this example, let's say the neighbourhood Police have an initiative to curb crime on railway property. The initiative has been developed due to recent injuries and a short presentation has to be developed for school assemblies. The format could be interpreted as:

1. Introductions (Who you are, why you are here)
2. How long the presentation will take.
3. The objectives, what the audience will learn? Three topics: The role of the Railway Police, the consequences of being on railway property and popular initiatives.
4. The main section
5. Opening statement to develop the first emotional response. "You may be aware of a recent

accident on the railway crossing where school children were injured, in a moment we're going to look at that situation and share the details with you..." The first sentence may create curiosity, intrigue or interest in some of the audience.

6. Topic 1, the role of the railway police. Set the frame, why are they interested? What do they do? You may deliver this information in an upbeat friendly manner, highlighting the positive aspects of the work.

7. Topic 2, the consequences of being on railway property. This is clearly a serious topic and the tonal content has to change. At this point in the presentation you choose to introduce fear, sadness, loss, emotional states that emphasise the enormity of injuries on the railway. Perhaps, one specific incident. Remember, you promised to inform them of this at the start of the presentation.

8. Topic 3, popular initiatives. Bring the energy of the presentation back on line. State the positives, be up-beat. Then close the story with a happy ending, perhaps the person that was injured was lucky, he made a remarkable return to good health.

9. The ending

10. Summarise, what you have just said.

11. Call to action. In this scenario, give the audience a web site or telephone number to call.

As you can appreciate this is a simplified version of a presentation. Just remember, make the transitions in emotion smooth and with a level of congruency that matches your intentions.

Fit in with the rest of the presentations

When you prepare, bear in mind that other speakers will make points and give examples in their section of the program. You won't need to completely rewrite your presentation, but be mindful that you want to look like a cohesive team.

Take time to listen to the other presentation during the run through period and real show. You never know, you may need to adjust what you say to make sure that it doesn't conflict with what has been said. I don't mean change your whole thoughts on a topic or cross your social boundaries. Just follow as if you are adding to the message that has already taken place and not arguing with it.

You will sound really knowledgeable if you refer to the previous speakers name and add emphasis to their points.

"As Michael explained earlier, keeping software up to date is really important. Let me show you where updates really help our product..."

SMILE - Method

The method dictates how you are going to get your message across. It's a container to package your words so that they become memorable to the audience. There are many ways and many methods, in fact the more imagination you use in creating your method, the more interesting it becomes for the audience. If it's interesting you will keep their attention, which is a hypnotic requirement (if you don't have their attention your objectives cannot be met) and send them away with an everlasting picture of your speech inside their minds.

The method also allows you to break down your information into smaller chunks that can be allocated a portion of time. Imagine if you had a full allocation of time and a raft of information to get over in the speech, it would be so easy for you to extend each topic and overrun. Whereas, the selection of methods I have drawn up here mean that you can insert small specific elements of information and rehearse them to a perfectly timed structure. Let's take a look.

The elevator pitch

The elevator pitch, so called as it relates to a thirty second journey you may have with a person in a lift and your ability to let them know about you, your products or services. An analogy can easily be drawn between any short presentation where you take turns to introduce your company or give out information. In thirty or sixty seconds you need to be able to get your message over congruently. Remember, you never get a second chance to make a first impression. The elements of the elevator pitch are:

- Your name
- The name of your company
- What you do

"My name is Steve Ashman of Alpha Blinds & Manufacturing in the UK. We are Europe's number one supplier of eco-friendly window blinds. You may have heard of us, our entire range of products look fantastic and are made from completely recycled plastics. Here is my business card, take a look on the web site."

Spoken out loud, this paragraph takes around 25 seconds if done in a conversational style. Remember, an elevator pitch is informative, but not a hard sell. As with the majority of presentations get the audience curious first. Let's break this down.

"My names Steve Ashman of Alpha Blinds & Manufacturing in the UK."

This is a perfect opportunity to create copious amounts of rapport, be friendly offer a hand shake.

"We are Europe's number one supplier of eco-friendly window blinds."

The point here, is to say something that catches their attention. Don't make wild inaccurate claims about your product, service or company. Be truthful or your sins will find you out. They may look on your web site, or do some digging to find out this isn't true and you will have lost their trust.   You can always find something interesting to say.

"We are a small family run butcher's shop, which means we really care about our customer."

The statements don't have to make you look big, they can portray sincerity, honesty, great service, organisation and structure. In fact, anything that reflects how you work.

"You may have heard of us, our entire range of products look fantastic and are made from completely recycled plastics."

Doesn't that sentence make you stop and think, that sounds interesting? I am not remotely interested in home furnishings and yet I have lifted my level of intrigue to a point where I would like to see this. Do you keep a picture in your pocket or on your phone?

"Here is my business card, take a look at the web site." Why not. A web site is the central hub of a business. You want to drive traffic to it. If you tweet, take the persons card and create an association.

#alphablinds are pleased to be associated with #corbymouldings

This will create even more traffic to the web site.

Here are a few more examples:

"My name is Robert Carter working for the Flash Courier Company, established originally in Birmingham, now with offices all around the UK. Our speciality is moving small items of high financial value from one secure destination to another. All of the big high Street Jewellers use our service. We stand by three things in our business. Speed, same day delivery and integrity, we only use our own security personnel."

"Hi I'm Maria Smith, probably best known for my chain of luxury food shops. I've found it really refreshing to create something that so many health conscious people want to be a part of.   I don't have a sales force, I rely entirely on word of mouth. Try my web site fabeats.co.uk."

The point of a short presentation as this is to excite the person, give them information and then allow then to speak. When they offer their company information, listen intently and ask questions. Engaging with the audience and allowing them to ask questions will cement a positive memory for future use.

There is one important factor with a short presentation. Write it down and learn it word by word, off-by-heart until you can recite it without fluffing the words. Don't sound as if you don't know what you are doing and mumble through the entire thing. Learn the words by saying them out loud, over and over. This is really important. By reciting the words out loud, you can build a speech pattern which is sharp and delivers on its promises.

My friend John

Storytelling (a hypnotic principle) is a perfect way to change the minds of the audience by stealth, instead of trying to bully them into seeing your side of an argument. People in general have a problem with anyone that tells them what to do. The advice might be sincere, heartfelt and downright useful, but we still resist the inference we are doing it wrong or could be doing it better.

At the start of this book I mentioned the phrase, the meaning of your communication is the response that you get. To recap, if we say or infer something and the person fails to change or take our advice on, it is our communication that is at fault, not the audience. Read these two paragraphs and decide which contains the more powerful and effective communication.

"I think your golf style is pretty good. You have a great swing and it's clear that you have worked on your technique. The only thing I would say to you is, keep your head down. If you do, the power you create behind the ball will lift your game. You'll do great."

"That's a great technique you have. It reminds me of my friend John. He took lessons from a world class professional at a golfing school in Florida because he really wanted to beat the competition. Do you know what the most important thing they told him? 'John you can really be outstanding at this sport if you do one simple thing. Keep your head down during the swing' and that's what he did and he beats me every time."

In hypnosis this is called the indirect method of communication. Take it from me, there are times when speaking directly is just as efficient as the indirect method – use them both. In the first example, you can imagine being the golfer's friend can't you. At first you use the pat, kick, pat philosophy. You pat the person on the head metaphorically and compliment them, then you add the somewhat sharper truth behind the situation and smooth things out with another compliment.

Direct communication can, if used inconsiderately, draw attention to the presenter and their views. It implicates the presenter in negative thoughts that the audience may feel. You could be seen as saying:

"I am right, you are wrong."

The second version, the indirect communication negates the speaker's opinion by making the words those of a third party, a professional or specialist. My friend John is a widely used and effective technique. It is advisable, whichever name or situation you stipulate that those people or things exist. Honesty will add congruency to your example and will ensure that future discussions will not expose your example as a lie, destroying the credibility you have built up along the way.

The magic story
This technique adds fire to your story telling abilities. A story if you are not careful can lack imagination and leave the audience feeling flat and lifeless. This is not a good situation for the professional presenter as we need to change the emotion of the person to get them to accept our ideas.

The magic story relies on the fact that whatever the subject you are going to discuss, it will always appeal to the listener. As you would expect, a structure exists that guarantees a positive result.

1. OPDS – Opening prime desire statement
2. Magic story
3. The guarantee

The opening message as we've already discovered is designed to create curiosity. It generally contains between 4 and 17 words, is short and can be spoken easily. In marketing terms it is a strapline that leads the listener towards something new and interesting.

- Ever wondered how to save money in your shopping bills?

- Want to know what the three important things all golf professionals do, that anyone can learn?
- A friend of mine has just returned from Madrid, boy did he have some stories to tell...
- Ever wonder how Mathew got that tattoo just before he got married?

It isn't a hard thing to do to deliver a line of this magnitude. A statement or question that gets the listeners creative juices flowing. The most important thing is, when you deliver the line you need to stop talking and look at the faces of the audience. Maybe nod knowingly, or lift your eyebrows or even lift your hands and show the palms of your hands. In exactly the same way as a hypnotist works, if the audience isn't listening, if you don't have their attention, if they haven't focussed in on what you just said, then don't say any more. What would be the point? You want their attention don't you?

Imagine a room of two hundred and fifty rowdy footballers screaming and shouting after the biggest win of their lives. Would you speak quietly and say:

"Excuse me gentlemen, would you mind being quiet, I have something to say."

Chances are, you won't be heard. Would you then go on to tell them that they have won a prize of a weekend's holiday? No. They wouldn't hear it, so you are wasting your time?

Start loud, get their attention. Wave your hands around to call order, then give your OPDS opening prime desire statement, so loud that everyone hears it and knows it's important. Now look at them. Do you see one person that isn't listening? Call them. Get them to face you. Got their attention? Deliver the message.

Now, on to the magic story. If your story is a Christmas tree, add baubles, tinsel, lights, add a fairy to the top. It's now magic isn't it? We so often forget how magical our world is. We get used to the world around us and forget exactly what contribution we made to it.

You may have been selling a product for years and know every feature of its makeup, inside and out. The customer however, may never have seen or heard of the item before. To them this is something new. When we are being sold to we spend a short amount of time at the start of the presentation trying to figure out whether the item is going to work for us. The in-built 'what will it do for me' is constantly running. It is at this moment that you can capitalise on your value.

Marketers use this methodology all of the time when advertising product.

- "This isn't just ordinary drinking water, this is water that fell on the Ulvearn Mountains in the South of France. Completely free of any additives, this drinking experience is filtered by rocks laid down over two million years ago to give you the finest, thirst quenching moments."

- "The Geebert Econo-Cycle is transport engineering at its best. Unrivalled in any field, the Geebert turns the ordinary bike ride into an amazing performance which will blow away the competition. Break with convention and do something crazy."

When you are talking about the life of a person in a eulogy, a product or service that you offer or even introducing an idea to friend, get enthusiastic. Emphasise the great bits and give your audience the chance to see themselves in the story. Use the phrases 'can you imagine', 'I wonder what would happen if' or 'can you imagine that'. Each time we see something new we like to build pictures in our minds, this closely associates the item or situation with us and essentially you have been sold.

Say a Ferrari goes past you down the road, what do you do? You whistle and your next thought is you inside that same car driving, imagining the possibilities. If you stop speaking even for a few moments, the mind will continue to build the picture making it more real for the audience. If you talk, you grab the attention of the speaker and the picture is lost, what a waste.

The magic story should be bright and display a complete success. Again, never lie. Outrageous claims will always be detrimental to your presentation.

The guarantee seals the deal. Everyone likes a guarantee. A guarantee is a way of removing the risk of doing or purchasing something. In the presentation it takes the pressure off. If you have been building up the benefits of your products in the audiences mind and are looking to close the presentation, I would suggest that the emotional journey at the end is on a high. The audience will be at the stage where they have to commit themselves to something. Whether it's to sign up for a product or service, let a friend know they wish to go on holiday, or offer a donation for a charity, it doesn't matter. Even if the commitment is valueless in terms of money, the guarantee can still be used.

As a company owner your aim has to be satisfied customers or your business won't survive too long, so if it's a product you are selling you could try.

- This product has a 30 day, money back guarantee. At any time in the next 30 days, if you are not completely satisfied with this product you can return the item along with its packaging for a full refund.

Now you may be thinking, this is crazy. Customers will return the product for no reason and I will end up with a massive amount of used stock. Really? In recent years, I've sold cosmetic and healthcare products which are at the dearer end of affordability. All of the products have a 60 day money back guarantee, even if the creams, potions, lotions or drinks have been consumed, the packaging can be returned for a complete refund.

This is guarantee by the manufacturer. It makes the home distributors comfortable and the end user. Then why doesn't the business fold like a pack of cards then? The products are the best. The manufacturer believes it, the dealers believe it and so do the end users. If they are sold ethically, to the right people with the right need, they do work and therefore returns are always minimal. A customer that returns a product is not black listed, but if they are consistently unhappy with the product then another sale need not take place.

Remember, a presentation is a congruent display of your feelings and words that match your body language. Be ethical, truthful and enthusiastic and people will believe in what you do. Snake oil sales people will always offer flimsy guarantees and bad news travels fast.

The guarantee doesn't have to be a monetary value though, it could be a swap for an alternative flavour or item in the product line. Say for instance, you are a restaurateur and you conduct a presentation to invite business owners to eat at your venue. Your guarantee could be:

- "I am pleased to announce that only the freshest, seasonal produce are used in my kitchen. So proud am I of this fact that any guest that cares to dine with me can visit the kitchen to see for themselves. We are always striving to be the best and it's your approval that counts."

Make them an offer they can't refuse, a promise or even a warranty that shows quality behind the brand you are building. Make the guarantee part of your unique selling points and lead with this information in every presentation.

The magic numbers
Certain hypnotic patterns have been used by marketers forever and they use them because they work. These patterns are simple and are really easy to remember. The magic numbers are 1, 3, 5 and 7. Try these for size.

- 3 steps to heaven
- Numero Uno
- Formula 1
- It's as easy as ABC
- 7 wonders of the world
- The 1, 2, 3 of presentation mastery
- 3 times a lady
- Hi 5

The list is pretty endless. When you think about these patterns in terms of presentation method, you can allow your message to hang on each number. Here are a few examples: In sales, you will often see a presentation rounded up with.

"Now that you are convinced that our product will make your life easier, there's only three things to do. 1.

Call today on the toll free number.   2. Select the size and colour that's right for you and 3. Feel safe in the fact that our 30 day money back guarantee ensures that you will only be charged if you are 100% happy with our product."

Reasons why you should attend a meditation class.

"Meditation is a truly mind expanding experience. When you leave our classes you will benefit from three things. 1. You will sleep better than you have in many years. 2. Your energy levels will soar and 3. The relaxation will add to your daily concentration making you more productive."

Weight loss motivation seminar.

"Include these five simple exercises into your routine and realise that your goals and dreams can be achieved. 1. Walk for 5mins extra every day. 2. Allow your heart to beat faster for twenty minutes, five times a week. 3. Always take a walk at lunch time to break up your day. 4. Take a friend with you on every walk. And 5. This is the most important factor in your weight loss, SMILE because you are loving it."

This simple practice of using magic numbers is easy if you use props or PowerPoint to emphasise what they are.

Be aware that if your presentation is a stand up talk without visual aids you may want to use numbers sparingly. It is so easy when you are in mid flow to get distracted and forget what one of the numbers means. Your subconscious mind doesn't take too kindly to the shock of wracking your brains trying to remember and it looks odd in the audience's eyes.

Acronyms and multiple letters

You can find this technique used everywhere in life. Even in this book I have used SMILE and PPP. When we try to learn something our minds look for association. So, why not create the association and apply it at the start. I've seen presenters that are teaching an audience create a pattern that they drill into the listeners.

In my sales training career, I created a training course on how to use return on investment to convince a customer to buy. I would explain that the return on investment method was like a mushroom and with every piece of justification we offered the customer, the bigger the opportunity would become. This is a bit like a mushroom growing in the ground, the longer you leave it to grow, the bigger it becomes. This is essentially an analogy or small story.

The way to learn the return on investment method was to take into account three elements in the acronym, CEP.

- Calculate – the facts and figures behind the ideas
- Effect – the reason the customer would spend his money
- Perception – how the client perceived the overall solution

Of course, CEP is another word or type of mushroom, another association. You will find years later that the acronym you use in your presentation is remembered long after the content of the presentation. Try to keep the acronym short, supercalifragilistic, probably wouldn't work unless the audience were Mary Poppins fans. If your word matches the topic or the themes of the day you have done very well. Thinking outside the box for a moment, if your theme was rockets, you could break it down into:

- Super
- Calibrational
- Fragile
- Ballistic

One of the pitfalls of an acronym is where you try to create a word by changing the original meaning of your pattern. Say the nearest word you can create is TANT and you want to create the word TENT. The A might stand for actual, where if you use a thesaurus the nearest E word is existing. Although similar, the meaning is somewhat different.

A simple solution to creating these words is to type your examples into Microsoft Word. Highlight your examples with the cursor and press Shift and F7 simultaneously. The online Thesaurus will offer many alternatives.

Tell a story

Fables have existing for thousands of years, handed down by story tellers throughout the generations so you know they work. A story encompasses the 'my friend John' technique. A message of great importance that can be hidden in the story that has a deeply profound effect on the listener without them knowing.

Stories come in all shapes and sizes. If you are presenting to a school group visiting a library, a story would be a perfect way to introduce new ideas. You cannot motivate anyone to learn unless they are in an up-time trance. Essentially you have to make them happy, positive and motivated before your message is accepted.

In the library scenario your objective may be to enthuse a new generation into reading books, allow them to explore the benefits of joining the library system and help them develop a healthy curiosity for new information. Let's take those three objectives and mould them into a story using emotional stepping stones as a vehicle.

The stages of the emotional journey will always differ depending on the audience. You will need to take into account the adverse effects of negative emotions on children for instance. You may choose.

- Curiosity
- Laughter
- Suspense
- Success
- Euphoria

Now apply the elements of the storyline to the emotional journey. The story could, of course, be a famous parable, characters from a well-known book or even a word for word rendition of a classic tale.

- Curiosity – before you open the book or begin the tale, do you have their attention? If you haven't don't proceed. Give a reason or two why you would like to read this story. The attention span of a child isn't long and a great presenter will always ask questions of the audience. '...and do you know what it was?' The moment you have their attention move on.
- Laughter – as you introduce the characters, heroes and villains of the piece, make the audience laugh. Create that up-time trance. Getting the children to boo at the right character is hooking their imagination.
- Suspense – This emotion is softer than fear, you may also choose challenge or hardship as emotions that match the type of people you are teaching. Lower your voice at this moment and make your audience listen. Slow down and even stop, silence will

emphasise your point.   The heroes are under pressure from the villains.

- Success – The heroes win out. Raise your voice, add positive emotion to your voice.
- Euphoria – What better way to get someone to remember your story by mimicking the celebration in the room. Cheering, Mexican wave, hoorah's.

You may be thinking, hold on a moment I am making an important speech to my peers on the importance of eagle hatchlings in the UK and creating an emotional journey hardly seems an appropriate way to approach this.

A story doesn't have to be childlike. In its simplest form, stories, parables or fables were used as an education. Before TV and radio had been invented, a story would carry an important message, often becoming legend and transforming with each telling.

When you are discussing a business issue the same rules apply.   Back to the eagle hatchlings for a moment. Let's say, the objectives in this case are that the numbers of mating birds are dwindling this year due to the theft of eggs and you want to raise funding for security and further research.

- Introduction – who you are, what you do and why you have a passion for this species.   Start with a positive, upbeat presence.
- Facts and figures – be specific, how many mating pairs were there last year and how many this year? Paint a picture, this a serious situation and you are an expert in this field.
- The results of doing nothing – Make this section a sombre experience for the audience. Show pictures of the devastation. Be specific, one particular case that is really sad. Tug at the emotional heart strings of the audience to affect change.
- Your impact on the situation – 'Of course, there is good news, with a team of dedicated volunteers...' Now is the time for you to say how your expertise will make the change.
- Turn your one success into euphoric strategy – Appeal for donations of money and time, get them to become a part of your organisation, how could they say no?

What you have created is a storyline. You've taken the audience on a journey, created trust, given them your credentials and shown them a new future. You may have embedded an important message in the text. It is a story about you. What stops you from applying this criteria to a best man speech? Or perhaps one company's department selling themselves to the rest of the company?

A story within a story

This technique is often used by master hypnotists as a way of hiding meaning in the words. It creates a confused conscious state that develops bewilderment and surprise. It lowers critical thinking and allows the message of the story to permeate the unconscious mind without being filtered.

In England in the 1970's, the Two Ronnie's reigned supreme. A comedy act mixing musical and situation comedy sketches. A weekly slot would be allocated to Ronnie Corbett who would sit in a comfy chair and recite a number of stories. These comic anecdotes were interlinked over a period of five or six minutes in the chair. The set was established like this.

- Start of story number 1
- Start of story number 2
- Start of story number 3
- End of story number 3
- End of story number 2
- End of story number 1

This process is masterful. It takes a lot of confidence to interlink and weave the messages you have created. I've often heard speakers open with a really positive statement saying something like.

"How are you all, have you had a great weekend? (Start of story number 1) I had a great time on Saturday, it isn't every day you get arrested, cautioned and blessed on one day. (Pause) Anyway, more of that later. I need to tell you about…. (This is the start of story number 2)"

At the end of the performance. Someone in the audience will shout out.

"So what did you get arrested for?'

The answer might be. "

"I saw a burglary, I stopped the man and the Police thought it was me. Later when they found out I wasn't the culprit I was commended."

You created so much curiosity on a subject at the start of the presentation that throughout your speech they were still able to remember it and were looking for the answer.

If you have a really serious topic to brooch with the audience, make it story number 3.   The start of the first and second stories will create enough emotion to allow the content of story 3 to take a smoother journey. By rounding off the topics in story 2 and 1 you make it harder for the audience to object or ask questions.

Personally, I wouldn't use this technique on your first outing as a presenter. It takes a lot of skill to perform and good memory to remember the sequence. Forgetting the end of a story would destroy the effectiveness of the technique. The audience would see this forgetfulness and associate it with negative congruency, depleting your trusted status. If you want to be a master of storytelling, practice, practice, practice.

Working as a team or duo
When you work as a team you must look like one unit, not two separate people talking in order. The issue here is nothing to do with the material you produce, it is more to do with the procedure you go through to rehearse. Recently I coached two business sales people who were experts in their field. They had written an informative collection of topics and had created a well-designed PowerPoint presentation. At the first run through they had divided the slides essentially odd numbers for one and evens for the other, with the intention of reading alternatively.

The effect was a staccato rhythm of words with no real purpose or impact on the audience. I will cover the theories of practice in the next section, only to say now that working as a team means so much more. Learn the whole presentation on your own first. Get to know the detail inside and out. It is useful to do this just in case your partner for whatever reason cannot make the live run through.

Allow the presentation to change every time you practice it out loud. It doesn't matter what you remember to say or what you don't, it is your enthusiasm and intention that will carry the message.

Put your notes down. Speak when you have something to say and listen intently. If you are using PowerPoint then allocate one person as the operator. When your partner makes a point, join them in offering assurance adding credence to your message.

Speaker 1: "The V-Hoover is unrivalled in its power."

Speaker 2: "It's a very strong feature of this machine, as you'll see in the Home and Garden magazine. In their showroom test, no other vacuum cleaner came anywhere close?"

In 2008, I worked with a colleague at the Exhibition Centre in Birmingham. We had fourteen presentations over two days, each of forty-five minutes. Our approach was to represent the technology company I worked for and a customer shown as a case study.

As the sales manager I introduced our business and the products we sold. The customer explained the original requirements and displayed the answers in terms of product demonstration and PowerPoint slides.   I was then in a position to talk about the reality of the situation all with interactive speech between the two of us.

The layout was simple. I stood on the left wearing a headset microphone and the second presenter, sat the other side of the presentation screen controlling a laptop on a small podium.   The effect was tremendous. After each performance it would often take 15 minutes to clear the room, so many people wanted to stay behind and speak to us about the detail.

SMILE – Imagination

It sounds obvious, use your imagination. But, what is imagination and how far are you willing to go to make your presentation memorable.   Do you want it to be professional, outlandish or funny? If you are scared of the presentation or the thought of the audience not liking what you say, you create imaginary boundaries that hold you in. A fear that by going too far or over stepping the mark, the audience will view your approach as uninteresting or garish.

By stepping out of the box, breaking the normal patterns that the audience expects and setting your sights higher than you can imagine will pay a fruitful bounty of appreciation. An audience is looking to be entertained and enthralled, not bored. Remember, if the audience know that this is your first presentation they will have a set expectation. Well now is your opportunity to prove them wrong.

In this section, we are going to look at how an idea is formulated from scratch and arranged for the highest impact. There are many tools you can use to do this, but I want to introduce you to a method that has worked for me for over ten years and is right beneath your nose.

Microsoft Word Outline

Read that line again, it doesn't say Microsoft Word, it says Microsoft Word Outline.   I remember the first time someone showed this to me. Just three minutes of tuition and I have used it ever since on every session of brainstorming.   When I write a book I use this to create the order of the chapters, for every stage hypnosis show where the material is specific to the audience and of course, for every presentation I am involved in. Follow these instructions carefully.

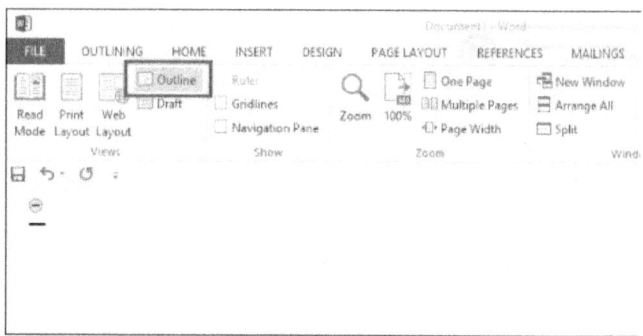

- Open a new, blank Microsoft Word template
- Before you type any words, click the View menu and select Outline (a cross will appear on the left hand side of the viewing area)
- Type Chapter 1 and Enter
- Type Chapter 2 and Enter
- Type Cats and Tab (notice that the whole line now in-dents)

In a few seconds you can begin to see a tree pattern evolving. You should now have three lines. The first two are the headings with the third nestled under Chapter 2.

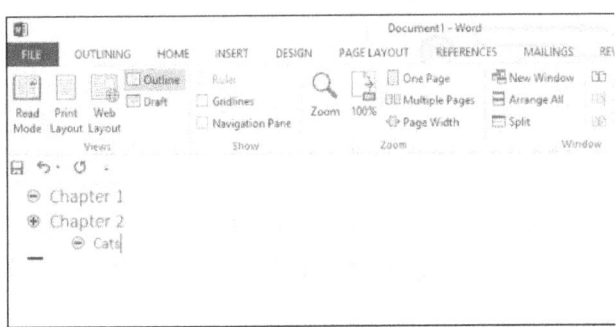

The real benefit of Outline is that you can quickly jot down all of your ideas into a list. This practice of brainstorming is a perfect way to stretch the boundaries of what you think is achievable. When all of the words are down in the list you can quickly begin to alter the order of each bit of information.

The features of Outline you should become accustomed with, are:

1. Press Tab to indent an entire line
2. Press Shift and Tab together to move the entire line to the left (un-indent)
3. To move a line up or down, left click on the Plus (+) or Minus (-) on the left of the line and drag to the required position
4. To collapse or expand a line, double click the Plus (+) sign on the left hand of the line
5. To move an entire section, collapse the section by double clicking the Plus (+) and move by dragging the Plus (+) to the desired location.

There are a number of other features available on the tool bar at the top of the screen which you can explore at your leisure, but it is that simple. As a tool nothing rivals the flexibility of Microsoft Word Outline and the chances are, you are using Microsoft Office and have always had access to this product.

I love the simplicity of Outline. You can have the entire document open and expanded or work with levels collapsed to make it easy to read. You can highlight sections and indent or move whole pieces of text in an instant. I know there is a highlight and drag feature in Word itself, but this is much easier. My advice is to stop and learn something new, this one piece of advice is worth the cost of this book alone.

Brainstorm ideas

Never lose faith in the fact that brainstorming is the most important part of the actual presentation process. If you are working alone or as a team this is not the time to have preconceived ideas. I've sat in so many board meetings where the seminar director has dictated exactly what he wanted from each performance. By all means set objectives. Know exactly what it is you are aiming for. Make sure that all of the presentations sit into a theme, but don't allow creativity to suffer.

Say for instance, that the company has commissioned a day for the seminar and you have been given one hour for your section. You now know what the message should be and you know what two other sections of the day you have to dovetail into. Now, start the brainstorm process.

If your team is five people, shout out ideas and DON'T criticise or analyse them. All ideas are good ones. I am going to play with the idea that we are working for an oil company, our session is on new techniques in production and the session directly before ours is on health and safety and the session afterwards is about profitability. Please bear in mind, I don't work in the oil industry and I am not an expert, so the ideas are just examples. Just remember that the same may be true in your party, new comers to the business and experienced hands should all be treated equally in this process.

Make sure you write everything down. (use Microsoft Word Outline)

1. Don't analyse how useful the idea is at this moment.
2. Don't criticise any of the team members or you will stop them from being interactive.

The finished result in Microsoft Word Outline should look something like this, only a lot longer.

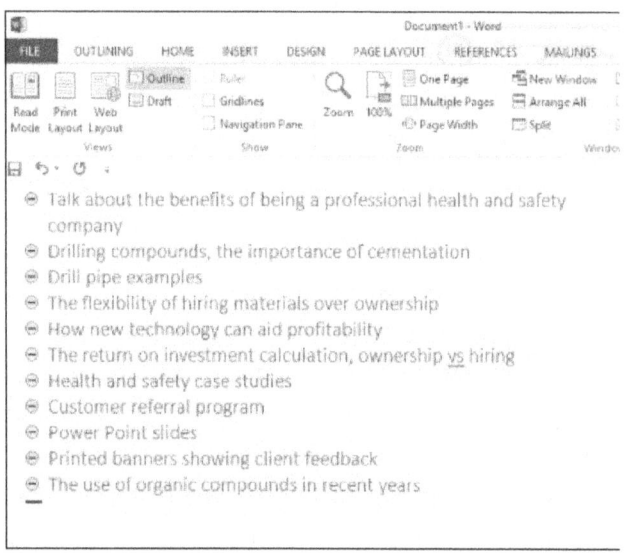

I know, this looks really complicated. A list of meaningless information that you would have no way of presenting. Good, that is exactly how it is supposed to be. Keep going, exhaust every last idea you have. Record everything, big ideas, how to present it, finite detail, just write it all down.

Now here comes the interesting part, putting the information into some sort of formality. I've already told you how to move and indent lines. Take into consideration the objectives of the presentation and within a few short minutes you should have something resembling structure.

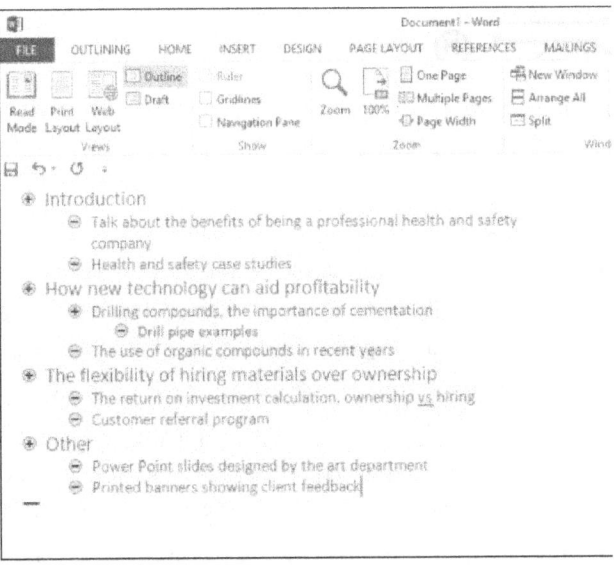

All of a sudden the piece has structure. By applying timings to each section you can now decide on the real detail. In this presentation example, it might ten minutes for the introduction and ten minutes for the summary, leaving twenty minutes for each middle section.

At first, an hour may seem a long period of time. Broken down though, you can easily begin to see that you won't need an enormous amount of content.

Developing a strong message
When you are brainstorming consider your own personal style. What kind of presenter do you want to be? Light hearted, funny, serious, etc. In this section, The Hypnotic Wisdom of Presentation Mastery will look at the nuances of style and how to adjust your preparation to give you the best chance of succeeding.

Being funny, telling jokes. For me, the stage comedian is one of the most professional presenters there is, hands down. It's a tough gig, not only writing funny material, but understanding the delivery and audience dynamics of comedy. This is an art form, packed with professionalism. Consider if telling jokes is you. Many a best man speech is thwarted by a misplaced or inappropriate pun. Of course, blue, cutting edge humour can, if delivered in the right way, engage an audience. However, an adverse reaction could mean disaster. I'm sure a Google search containing a topic and the word joke will bring up many off the shelf examples.

Tel them what you are going to tell them, tell them and tell them what you told them. We all learn by repetition. Remember, those days at school learning your times tables. Over and over until you knew them by rote. Hypnosis is exactly the same. A hypnotist will always repeat a phrase two or three times to ensure that the suggestion has sunk in to the subconscious mind of the hypnotee.

This technique should be used at the start, middle and end of your presentation. Try:

"Ladies and gentlemen, in the next fifteen minutes you will learn the important benefits of technology on this industry, gleamed from over five years of research and what it means to your profitability."

(Then, later during the detail)

"As I said earlier this detail proves that these working procedures will dramatically improve safety, cut cost and generate you more profits."

(At the end of the presentation summarise)

"...and here are the facts. Years of research and happy customers that are building greater opportunities in their business. We look forward to doing the same for you."

You don't have to say the exact words on each occasion, it is the message that is important.

Props. PowerPoint, although brilliant as a product this is not the only prop you can use. If every other presenter in the day is using PowerPoint, give the audience a break. The words 'death by PowerPoint' are all too true. Can you imagine using:

- A costume
- Music
- A pre-recorded soundtrack that you mime to, for fun
- Large printed pictures
- A whiteboard
- A telephone
- Inflatable toy, large telephone, a banana
- Disco lights

Out of context, a prop seems ridiculous. Apply that prop to a scenario and you are making a visual statement that can be remembered. If you are talking about profitability, a briefcase full of fake money would be interesting and funny.

The win-win choice should always be taken into account. Is the message you are delivering a one sided benefit? To get somebody on board with your idea they have to be able to see what's in it for them. Be careful and emphasise the benefits to both parties.

The yes set. The yes set is an agreement frame, a way of conditioning the mind to accept your proposal. Often used in sales, the theory is that a more complex idea is easily accepted if cushioned by normally accepted behaviour. So let's say you have to increase your prices which is a difficult subject.

- Topic 1 – something that is true and easily accepted
- Topic 2 – something that is true and easily accepted
- Topic 3 – something that is true and easily accepted
- Price increase information

The conversation may sound like this: (this is a shortened and detail-less version)

Topic 1.
"As you can appreciate our company has done all it can to maximise the number of sales leads that have been deployed to the channel in recent years. An increase of 20%." (This is true and cannot be disputed)

Topic 2.
"The business is launching a new marketing campaign on TV and radio this year that we will all benefit from." (It might not be new information, but is it good news)

Topic 3.
"I am pleased to announce a new member of staff to help with customer service this year."

Price Increase information.

"It is our intention to increase the price of the following products...,(the reasons) etc."

In the hypnotic and NLP (Neuro Linguistic Programming) world this is called pacing and leading. You cannot truly ask someone to follow your way of thinking until you have acknowledged their own opinions and feelings.

I often give this rather bizarre football related example. If two supporters of rival clubs were cheering their teams on in a pub, what chances would one person have to sell the other a football club shirt? Let's face it, this is bizarre. You can see that there would be a vehement mistrust between the two people which in normal circumstances would not lead to a sale taking place. One party needs to change their behaviour to make something happen.

"I appreciate you support the Black Football team, I have to hand it to you, your manager really is highly skilled."

This is an unlikely phrase and maybe not in fitting with a real life scenario, but the meaning of the statement has the ability to change perception (pace) the listener's reality. Or what they perceive to be reality. You may choose a number of these statements to free the persons critical thought. You could add:

"Three wins in a row is a pretty outstanding achievement against the best clubs in the country."

Cognitive change is already happening, what we are waiting for is an indication that behavioural change has taken place. This may come in the form of verbal appreciation, a head nod or a statement of reciprocity perhaps.

The reply, "I appreciate that, both our teams are quite remarkable."

Now, you can go for the close, ask for the sale, you are now leading the audience towards your way of thinking.

SMILE – Less is more

You may now need to do a double take. Didn't I just tell you that you should write everything in your head down in Microsoft Word Outline? I clearly said, Brainstorm. Let your imagination run wild. We then sorted that information and found structure. In this section of SMILE we need to consider the audiences abilities to learn.

The speed at which people speak can loosely be used to indicate the speed of their learning. Take the example of when you join a new company. On the first day the HR person introduces you to an ensemble of new faces and processes to learn. At the end of the first day you are accomplished and have a pretty good idea how to get you started. It isn't until the first problem hits your desk that the information you learned day one becomes relevant and you realise you have holes in your needed repertoire.

What would have been a better and more efficient introduction to the company?

Maybe a hand-out with a seating plan, the name of the people and what their primary role in the organisation is. Perhaps slowing down, turning the whirlwind tour into an exercise with development examples. Maybe conducting the tour a second time allowing you to regurgitate what you had uncovered.

A presentation is the same process, use these three filters to refine your content.

- Repetition
- Speed
- Clarity

Repetition is the mother of all learning. Keep repeating the key point over and over. Each person's convincer strategy is different, but the more times you say something, the more chance it has of being remembered.

There are two ways you can do this. You can either say exactly the same words over and over or change the phrasing and allow your sentences to mean the same thing. Repetition is used in hypnosis to secure the suggestion, it works the same in normal language. Let's take the example of the times table, conventionally you would get the audience to recite the numbers by paraphrasing. 1 x 2 = 2, 2 x 2 = 4, etc. When you finally begin to hear a confident response you may mix up the proceedings by asking, "What are 2 x 4's?"

If you are teaching the audience a piece on health and safety, it is important they are able to repeat the words once you are gone, it may be something like.

"SOS stands for, stand back, open all windows and send for help."

This is a simple acronym to aid learning, but effective.

The speed in which you deliver the information, greatly dictates the amount of material you can deliver. Think about speed in the same way you alter your tone in developing emotion. Speed and silence used in alternating unison are more impactful than a continuous stream of information. When you begin to practice, sip water between each section and get used to the silence.

Clarity. The clearer you make something, the easier it is for the audience to remember it. If you have a complex subject to cover, you need to make it easy. Create a story or a metaphor. I attended an employee day for one of the dealerships I was working with. Each department took time to explain what they did in turn. Even though the company wasn't overly large, thirty employees or so, it was amazing how little was known about each other's objectives. The IT department went on to discuss their role in the management of servers and desktop PC's and duly named each piece of equipment after the characters in the TV comedy, Friends. The relationship between IT servers and TV characters may not be easily apparent now, but at the time all of the employees enjoyed the programme and found the associations clear to understand. It made the presentation memorable and interesting. As you can imagine the PowerPoint slides were adorned with pictures from the show as an added benefit. (Beware of copyright infringement.)

When you are developing material you have to think about your audience.   If the people listening are technically competent individuals then raise your game and introduce technicality. Just remember to tone these technical elements down when an overview for lay people is required.

PowerPoint is the most emotive of subjects when it comes to presentations. It is one of the most flexible and useful pieces of software a presenter can use, as long as they follow some important guidelines.

1. Don't pack the slide with too many words.
2. A picture does paint a thousand words.
3. Don't animate for interest sake.

4. Allow the audience to read the slide before moving on.
5. Avoid death by PowerPoint.
6. Create a master slide set and stick to it.
7. Don't look at the slides when you are speaking.
8. Test the clicker.

So many times I've sat in rehearsals and realised the presenter has decided to notate everything they are going to say in the slide. They then proceed to read the slide to the audience word for word, this is boring.

First of all, let's give the audience credit, they can read the words on the slide quicker than you can say them. If you read the slide, the sound from your mouth is stopping or at best interrupting the concentration of the reader, so they can't fully listen or read and take the words in.

Think about this scenario for a moment. You go to bed early for a change because you want to read the last few chapters of a really exciting book. Not wanting to be left alone, your partner comes to bed and puts the telly on. The sound from the TV and occasional conversation distracts your reading. You are neither giving your full attention to the book or the TV or the conversation and they all suffer.

Let's say I wanted my presentation to be about unity, the power of the community to combat crime and the benefit of being someone's best friend in a time of need. The PowerPoint slide does not need to reflect these words. It could be a picture such as a white dove or handshake, a symbolic gesture. It could display a quote from someone respected for their thoughts on peace, the Dalai Lama, Martin Luther King or Gandhi for instance.

"Live as if you were to die tomorrow. Learn as if you were to live forever." Mahatma Gandhi

Make the words large enough to be read easily, in a colour that is easy on the eye and don't add animation.

Now, as a presenter you hit the keyboard and the slide appears. For the first ten to fifteen seconds, be quiet. Yes, be quiet, say nothing at all. Give everyone in the room time for them to read and digest the words. It is your job to look out into the audience and see the emotional shift. These words will make emotional change which is what we want. It will be minor. You will need to be vigilant to look for a shift in the audience. They may sigh, take a deep breath and let their breath go or change what they are looking at. When you see this change in the majority of your audience, it is time to unleash your OPDS, your opening prime desire statement.

"Ladies and gentlemen, for this community to succeed, it needs to survive and we can only survive if we learn from our mistakes and push forward with our plans for growth."

Take a breath. At this moment you should be looking out into the audience to ensure you have their full attention.

"I am pleased to be asked to speak today because the people in this room can really make a difference….."

Notice, how PowerPoint is used as a supporting tool, not the main event. PowerPoint cannot create emotion in the same way that the human voice can. By adding space in the way of silence, you have created dynamic tension. This tension primes the unconscious mind to receive the next lot of information you are about to deliver.

One of the downsides of cramming too many words on the slide is that you lose the flexibility you have as a speaker. If you put twenty one numbered points on the slide you may feel obliged to mention each one. You won't be able to help yourself, as you read every word. As we'll discuss in the practice session, it doesn't matter what information you tell them and it doesn't matter what you forget to tell them, it is the quality of what you do say that will carry your presentation forward.

A picture paints a thousand words. In place of a quote or similar wording you may choose to create a visual representation of the information. This is good from a number of stand points. Firstly, the way that people learn is governed by their primary representation system, either visual, auditory or kinaesthetic. Smells and tastes also play a part.   By using pictures you are accommodating the visuals and by speaking the auditory learners are included. Nothing stops you from adding a kinaesthetic element either.   Kinaesthetic really means feel. Let them touch the end result or the product.

Secondly, the minds of our audience will build their own pictures from the information we give them. This is important. We set an objective for our presentation and we are slowly building a picture of success in the audiences mind. When they leave can they see themselves donning a uniform and being part of the community wardens? Maybe they can if your description and emotional message relates to their intentions to do something good.

I have said, don't animate for interest sake, but nothing stops you from building a montage of relevant pictures that change slowly.   Set up an automatic timer so that you can continue to talk without being distracted.

PowerPoint has many animation features which allow the text and images to bounce and swirl and flash.   For your own sake, minimise their use. Too many images in motion will create confusion and that will only detract from your purpose. If you need to emphasis a word or recap on the acronym or press the call to action statement, then animation will offer much needed focus.

By now, you will have eliminated the next problem which is allow the audience to read the slide before moving on. Especially in business presentations when you want to make a point or give specific data. You may want to show a web address and you will see the interested audience members making notes on a pad. More often than not, these notes are recorded or photographed on a tablet device. If it's important, display the information and stand to one side to let them get it recorded. You may even ask them:

"Have you all made a note of that?"

A little audience participation goes a long way.

I love the phrase 'death by PowerPoint' because it dictates exactly what it is. The strange thing is, when we watch a presentation and we see too many slides we all use this comment, 'death by PowerPoint'. But, when we write our own slides we are just as guilty. Remember, be critical and keep it simple.

What you have to realise is, sitting in the audience is a completely different experience from giving the presentation. When you give the presentation there is adrenalin running, you are apprehensive at the start and when you get into the flow you create your own human emotion, a mixture of excitement and feeling good. So you think it's going great. When you sit in the audience you are sitting still and attempting to hold focus.

Concentration for 100% of the time is really hard work and you can't help your mind wandering. Slide after slide, after slide is hypnotic way of sending you to sleep!

Mix it up. Do something completely different to the rest of the presenters. If all the audience can remember is the number of slides, you have wasted your time.

Make a slide master. The slide master is part of the functionality of PowerPoint that is always discarded. You can have so much fun designing funky text and animated pictures that the slide master and formality of a design brief shoot straight out of the window. Again, if you are part of a larger team giving a large presentation, failing to use the slide master can result in a mish-mash of poor design.

What is the slide master?

The slide master is the part of the software that allows you to define what fonts, colours, sizes and background are appropriate in the design brief. The slide master set holds a separate design for each of the slide types, major heading, sub heading, detail slide, picture slide etc, there are a dozen or so of these slide master templates and you can add more.

When you add a new slide, the template is automatically picked up from the slide master set. So when you type your own words, bullet points and headings they all look the same. This is particular useful when amalgamating work from different presenters. Just beware, it doesn't take into account free form text boxes that have been added manually.

Don't look at the slides when you are speaking. Keep your face towards the audience. Nobody would pay to see the back of a pop stars head on stage, would they? When you turn around and read a slide you instantly lose connection. You also miss the opportunity to see what the audience are doing. The favourite things are missing the buying signal, seeing someone nod when you say something they like and worse when they don't like what you are saying.

If there are too many words on the slide you have to turn around because you will never remember what they are. The second thing that happens is, the volume of sound is reduced by 75%. So for one second the audience can hear you clearly and then you turn towards the screen and the sound falls. You only need a slight distraction in the room and the audience has missed what you said.

I sat in a presentation in Glasgow once, just off St Georges Square. It was a hot summer evening and they had installed a rotary electric fan beside the open window at the back to blow air into the room. An electric fan isn't particularly noisy, although a low hum has a surprising effect on the impact of the presentation. If the presenter at the front of the room doesn't project their voice forward, then those people at the back of the room will have a problem hearing. The low hum of the fan makes the whole presentation almost inaudible. Not being able to hear clearly is a sure way of turning people off.

Sometimes in seminars, a company will use tables at the back of the room to display product and company literature which can be browsed during the breaks. If you employ staff members to man these areas, make sure that you coach them to be silent during the actual presentation. It isn't always apparent on the stage that chatting at the back of the room is a major distraction.

Test the clicker. When operating PowerPoint you can advance the slide by pressing the keyboard, using the mouse or having an optional USB clicker. These things always work when you are rehearsing and seem to play up when the real event takes place. Give this a good test before you begin.

SMILE – Evaluate
Before you start to practice this wonderful material you have created, ask yourself the following questions.

- Are you achieving the objectives you have defined?
- Are you getting your message across in the cleanest way, for the most clarity?

- Is there too much information for the time you have?

The reason you are doing this presentation is because of the objectives. If you don't achieve the objectives, what is the point in spending all this time?

Rewrite the content to make it as simple as possible. The sooner your audience learns the message the sooner they will be on board with your idea. An unclear message creates procrastination.

When you start to rehearse your material, you will soon recognise if you have too much. Never be scared to go over one piece of material in the presentation until it is drilled into the unconscious thoughts of your audience. So many of us look for new material all the time, when you may be serving your audience better by sticking to a foundation topic and do it well.

Section 2 – Practice
The performance elements

If you have read the first page of the book and decided I want the number one tip of how to be a presentation master, then this is the only page you need to read. The number one tip for a great presentation is (drum roll please):

Do it out loud!

Are you doing a double take right now? Skipping back to the paragraph above to make sure you read the statement, because this is the number one presentation technique. This is it, four little works do it out loud. These four words are so powerful. Let me explain.

I know you are intelligent, because you have decided to get better at being a presenter. You've invested the money and time to read this book. As you are reading the book now, you are absorbing the words on the page and creating pictures in your minds. The spoken word is a presentation, images in your mind are not. This is important.

I've said all along that it is your role as a great presenter is to create images, sounds and feelings including emotions in the minds of the audience, but this will not help you practice your material. Read the following phrase in silence in your head.

"Good evening ladies and gentleman, it is indeed a great delight to see so many eager and welcoming faces in the audience."

Now say the same phrase out loud.

"Good evening ladies and gentleman, it is indeed a great delight to see so many eager and welcoming faces in the audience."

Now, I would hope you can feel, if not hear a difference.

- Does the text flow better in your mind or out loud?
- Does the phrase get straight to the point?
- Can you say all of the words without running out of breath?

There is no point writing a speech and relying on the actual performance to do it out loud for the first time. A great performance is a congruent performance, where your words match your intentions. This only comes from confidence and if you stumble over your words then confidence seems a million miles away.

In the early days of my career in sales I attended a seminar where the local tax office gave a thirty minute speech on the latest taxation measures. The two speakers, clearly competent and skilled in their respective roles had obviously never attempted a presentation before. Whilst one person read notes the other operated PowerPoint. The lack of confidence can easily be perceived as incompetence in the person, when really it comes down to one thing, you need to do it out loud.

Your mind has a convincer strategy in anything you learn. You may have heard the phrases consciously incompetent, unconsciously incompetent, consciously competent and unconsciously competent. These are the stages we go through as we learn anything. When you first get your new driving licence in the post you have no skill or competence at all. Then you learn to drive and every manoeuvre you make you have to consciously think about it (conscious incompetence). Of course, when you've been driving for a few years your unconscious mind takes over (unconsciously competent). This is a state where you are so confident you can use your phone and listen to music while you drive.

The same learning process is applied to presentations. With every rendition you make of the words out loud the better it will be come. As a convincer strategy you will begin to create your own idea of how much is enough. For me, I need to practice out loud at least four times to deliver sufficient confidence for the audience to buy in to my credibility.

You now have your Microsoft Word Outline document you prepared with your format and sections. I recommend you print this out. Beware page numbers are not visible when you do this, so you may want to manually number each page after printing. Don't think that it is a good idea to hold these in your hand while you rehearse. If you hold them in your hand you will suffer from projection issues. You will develop a technique where you always look down at the paperwork instead of beaming your speech out to the far reaches of the audience.

You could tape or Blu-tack the sheets in order to a rehearsal wall or to a white board at head height. You may even utilise a music stand, as long as the height of the sheets can be adjusted accordingly. This is the same technique I use when developing a new stage hypnosis show. There are around eighteen to twenty A4 sheets of words and format for each show and I tape these to a large white board. I lift this onto the arms of an office chair when I want to practice with the sheets at eye level.

The practice runs
   1. The first run through
   Your Word Outline is, in the main, is a list of ideas in bullet point form. It may contain a few specific things that you want to say, such as quotes or the like, but it is not a script. A great presenter may use acting skills, but this is not Shakespeare. You do not need to speak your Word Outline in a word-for-word fashion. The flavour of the content is what is required.

If you are an actor you have to respect the literary masterpiece of an author and articulate the exact words in a specific way. Acting is a fascinating and awe inspiring art form that is developed over a long period of time. This is not the presenter's art.

For you to give a presentation, you need to know the subject matter. Whether it's a product you sell as a company or a few words about a mate you worked with, you need to know the subject matter. In fact, you are the specialist on the subject, the trusted advisor.

Go to page one of the outline, this contains the introduction, the opening prime desire statement and your objectives for the duration of the presentation. You might have written "Ladies and gentlemen" and all of its supporting words in long hand and want to emulate this or you might have simply written the note 'the start'.

Stand up and present your introduction. Present is different to talk. Try on the words. Given them a go.

"Good morning ladies and gentlemen, my name is Steve Ashman and I'm here today to let you know our companies development intentions of the Thunderbolt 2000."

You will at this point, splutter, stall, choke, have varying levels of volume and of course, spaces in all the wrong places because you keep looking back at the paper. Brilliant you are well on your way to be a master presenter.

Do the same with each bit of text. Play with the words. At this point you may want to grab a pen and start playing with the mistakes you will invariably find. You may be using PowerPoint or have props, have these to hand to use while coordinating the words, it will all be clunky at the moment. Continue until you have talked through all of your sheets.

Well done, your first run through is complete and now we can work on making it perfect.   Remember, normal presenters get up to speak and this is the first time they say the words out loud, you are one step ahead already.

2.   The second practice run
Find a stopwatch on your phone. Before you speak again, set the stopwatch running so that at the end of the practice run, you can begin to get an idea for how long the entire outline takes to perform. At first you will be massively out. I've often seen presentations that should take 45 minutes, take only 15 minutes in the first runs, this we can work on.

At the end of the second run, how much more confident do you feel?

You are still relying on the paperwork and this needs to stop now. This is controversial. I was asked earlier in the year to help two sales people prepare for a corporate presentation where they were given 60 minutes to discuss around six topics. Soon after starting the practice, I complimented them on how knowledgeable they were and proceeded to bin the sheets of paper used for preparation.

One of the presenters protested, "But, I need to get my head round this stuff!"

The other chimed a similar line, "I need to go over this 30 or 40 times in my head before doing it live!"

My answer was simple. Both of these individuals had worked for the company for over eight years. Quite simply they were knowledgeable people that the audience, some of whom were customers, would instantly recognise their abilities. For years they had stood in front of prospects and customers alike in their offices on a one-for-one basis and offered all manner of highly technical solutions to business problems. These presentations were not scripted. So, why when you stand in front of an audience do you need to clutch to your safety blanket?

Often when I give a course on presentation mastery, I will ask for a volunteer in the audience who hasn't worked for the company for too long.   The shorter the time they have been employed the better in fact, a matter of days is desirable. The person remains in the audience and I ask:

"Can you tell me, do you have a hobby you are passionate about?"

When they respond with a yes, I ask a few questions about the hobby and get a conversation going. Without evening knowing it, they are already giving a presentation.

They may be shy, but they know about the subject and are comfortable.

Then I say,

"Sorry I need to change the camera angle, can you come up here please?"

I remain on the stage and we continue to talk and remain interested in each other so the audience can see. Then I take a seat in the person's seat and continue to listen. We continue this until it dawns on the audience that this is a confident, professional presentation. No nerves, a clean performance.

Why do we suddenly change our whole body language and approach when we think of the idea of a presentation?

If you are using PowerPoint as a prompt for you and the audience, then a simple set of bullet points from your Microsoft Word Outline can be entered in each slide, you don't need the paper. If you aren't using PowerPoint, then now is the time to create a set of small prompt cards. Keep these simple. Number each one at the top and add two or three bullet points to each one. They are useful if you need to know what comes next, you can simply glance down catch the phrase and begin to talk about it.

3. Building confidence

So, with all of the paper, the Word Outline now put to one side (we will need it to make refinements later, so don't throw it away) and your cue cards or PowerPoint in situ we can begin. Glance at the first slide or card and begin to speak. Say the first card or slide contains the words:

- Who am I?
- What do I do?
- The reason why I'm here?

Don't read the words, ad lib around them. I mean ad lib, because every time you do this presentation the words will be slightly different. It doesn't matter what you put in, or what you leave out, it is the overall impression that you make that matters.

When you have been practicing out loud for a period of time and as you become more competent, you will be able to allocate an allotted time to each section or slide. An average introduction of this nature should be around five minutes. Remember to be clear, bright and enthusiastic while you are in presenter mode.

By this stage of rehearsal, say the third or fourth occasion you will find the erm's are beginning to leave your voice.   The erm's in your conversation are created by your conscious mind looking for the next thing to say. This tells the audience that you are in confident or unsure. Each run through will allow your self-esteem to soar and your unconscious mind takes over and the words run freely.

Be on the lookout for words that you repeat too often when you speak. You may hear yourself saying words like 'basically' or 'which means that' at the beginning of each paragraph. This can be off putting for the audience. Now is the time to substitute these repeats, be creative.

The downward spiral
Beware of the downward spiral and its effect on the audience. I first discovered this effect when asked to be a best man at my friend's wedding when I was just seventeen. At that point, I hadn't actually been to a wedding and didn't know what to expect. I hadn't stood up and spoken to any sort of audience, even at school. My social skills with adults were almost zero and failed in the area of confidence.

I sat on the top table with very little preparation or plan, being looked at by a room of over a hundred people who stared at me as I stood up.   I remember as I first spoke, the tables closest to me, I now realise as close family and their partners all sat silently waiting for my words. Further back in the room, other friends and work colleagues, continued to enjoy each other's company and talked, creating an imbalance.

You see, from that moment on, the downward spiral had begun. I hadn't taken control and I certainly hadn't grabbed the attention of everyone before I unleashed the speech.   You sometimes see at a formal wedding, a Maître d take the floor who gains focus by rapping the wall or calling for order, this is a god send.

The downward spiral begins like this.

1. There is noise in the room
        This noise distracts the listeners from listening to you. At first it is merely annoying to the audience members that are listening. At a wedding you will even hear the close family verbally shushing the people that are making the distraction. This rarely happens in a business context.
2. Misunderstanding
        If the audience doesn't hear everything clearly and cannot create a cohesive clarity in the words, the message you offer is misunderstood. You can imagine can't you, a question at the end of your pitch that shows the mismatch of information. "Doesn't this product work on the UK's 240 volts supply?"
3. Scepticism
        If the distraction in the room continues, scepticism prevails. Inside the mind of the audience they may be thinking, 'I couldn't make a commitment to this company, I'm not sure they can do what I want.' An audience is a fickle master, they won't always tell you what they don't like. Not everyone is comfortable putting

their hand up and asking a question in case they are made to feel uncomfortable or humiliated.

4. Boring

Too much confusion. The inevitable result is fidgeting and boredom. This is a downward trance. You cannot motivate them when they are in a negative state of mind. At this point you have completely lost the audience.

When the downward spiral takes hold, it is almost impossible to bring the presentation back to normality. So, it is important you follow these steps:

- Stand up and get in the line of sight where everyone can see you.
- Make a noise that grabs there attention (clap loudly, shout, whistle, blow an air horn) or ask someone to introduce you loudly.
- Make sure everyone in the room is paying attention.
- Correct your volume, set a pleasant pace, develop copious amounts of interest and keep it relevant.

There is no point whistling and making a noise, if you don't draw the attention of the audience directly to you. Get out of your chair and let people see you. You could tap a wine glass with a knife making a chinking sound. This is often used to draw attention, but although I have never seen this fail it would be rather embarrassing if the wine glass broke in your hands. Starting your presentation on a back foot is a not a good idea.

When you stand up, be confident. Wave to the people at the back, especially if you don't know them. You are important now, this is your time to shine. You can make light of being so brash, as long as you get their attention. Why not, blow a referees whistle and then say:

"This is a yellow card, anyone that speaks while I am speaking will get one. Misdemeanour twice and the red will cost you a drink at the bar."

Do you think you will have their attention?

If someone in the room is speaking when you have brought things to order, be quiet and look at them. The glares from you and the rest of the audience will embarrass them to stop talking.

You can of course, use the 'My Friend John' technique we discussed earlier. This works especially well in a large audience. Imagine you are in a large ballroom and it's a Christmas party and as the organiser you need to give everyone important messages before they leave their tables and begin dancing. You can imagine that alcohol has already been consumed and getting your voice over the din is a challenge. Imagine these words.

(Talking to the group in the audience that are listening, the front two tables)

"I heard a great story about Bob Harris, the CEO at my last organisation. He bought a picturesque property on the banks of the River Trent and after the stress of the year he planned to holiday there over the summer. Well the summer came and on the first morning he was awaken by an incredible din. Do you know what it was?"

"Turkeys!"

"Thousands of them making a din right outside his window.   Well this went on for days and days until one morning he'd had enough and I mean enough. With enough whiskey in him to sink a battleship, he opened the window and shouted."

(Now shouting at the top of your voice)

"Shut up you TURKEYS!"

Now, if you had been listening and maybe you knew Bob, it would have sounded a really funny anecdote. For the unsuspecting talkers who heard, "Shut up you TURKEYS!" the meaning would have been entirely different. Either way you now have them in the palm of your hand.

Moving on the stage
Your body language is a big part of the congruency of a presentation.   If you have a video camera or a long mirror while you rehearse this is a good thing. As yourself, how do you stand? Is it upright with your shoulders back or do you slump your shoulders? Your stance is what sets a positive and enthusiastic person apart from a person in the dumps. A hypnotherapist can

change the demeanour of a stressed or upset client by simply raising where they focus their eyes and by sitting back in the chair. It is almost impossible to feel sad if you put your shoulders back, try it.

As a presenter, you do not need to stand still when you talk, unless of course, your company has supplied a lectern and you are tied to the spot.   You can walk about. Move from one side of the stage to another, move right up to edge of the stage or even sit down on the edge it is up to you.

PS.   Don't fall off the stage, when the lighting engineer makes the room dark. The only no-no is don't turn your back on the audience.   You won't see the reaction the audience are making to your suggestions. When you watch the weather man or women on the news in front of the map of isobar systems and rain, how do you feel when they lose eye contact with the camera and turn towards the map? The same things happens when the speaker turns to a PowerPoint slide and points at the text.

What are you going to do for half an hour with your hands?

Telling a story and using hand gestures makes it all the more visual and reassuring. Standing with your hands in your pockets may tinge the presentation with less commitment. I spoke about the use of silence earlier. You could hold a glass of water and take a sip when you have made an important point. The sip of water may only take a few seconds, just enough time for them to absorb the message in its entirety.

Don't read notes

If you have followed my rehearsal instructions you will know that the format and words of the presentation can change slightly with each rendition. What information you put in and what you leave out are less important than the way it is presented. So, you do not need all of the notes with you. If you are using PowerPoint slides the small number of words or pictures you have included on the slide will trigger your memory with something to say. By practising out loud and using repetition you will develop the ability to flow between concepts.

If you don't have PowerPoint or are at a wedding you may use a small stack of postcards to prompt the individual topics you want to cover. In the early days of using PowerPoint I would always have a card with bullet pointed topics in the breast pocket of my shirt as a backup device, although with commitment to practice out loud I never needed it.

Do a trial run with an audience

The audience you can muster at home may not know anything about the topic that you discussing. This is better for you. If an uninformed audience is convinced by your presentation, then the real audience will be too. Ask them to make notes and listen to the whole presentation before they ask questions.

At the end, ask their advice. Importantly, be quiet and listen to what they say, there may be some nuggets of real gold. All advice is good advice. Advice is a subjected opinion. They can only tell you what they saw and heard. This viewpoint may be entirely different from the real audience. Take on board what they say, be critical of your presentation and make changes. If you are part of a larger seminar, request that the whole group do a run through together. Sit in the audience and listen to what they say and do. Adjust your work to complement their presentations.

Look like a cohesive team and the audience will believe they are buying into an organisation that can deliver on its promises.

Make mistakes and move on
What is a mistake?

Most of the things that you associate with a mistake are in your mind only. You may fluff some lines or have paused a little longer than you had practiced or moved on to the wrong PowerPoint slide by accident. Let me tell you these are not mistakes. They are only perceived as mistakes by you. Remember, the audience has no idea what you are going to say. In fact, every practice run you have done has been different every time you've done it, so neither do you.

Nobody in the audience is looking for perfection that is what an actor strives for. If these things happen, make the correction and move on.

A real mistake would be telling the audience that the item you are selling is £10 and it is really £15. These honest mistakes do happen from time to time, even if you have rehearsed over and over.   Words can just slip out. Hold your hands up and apologise sincerely.

"I'm sorry, I've made a mistake, I should have said….."

No one will think any less of you, in fact the honesty to correct your content will only help your cause.

Equipment and room layout
Microphones
These are a useful addition to presentations. However, if you've never used one before the effect of amplification on the voice can pose new challenges and additional need for rehearsal. On a professional stage set up for actors or musicians, the sound is fed back on to the stage using back line monitors, so that the performer can hear themselves speak. The volume and balance of sound are not always the same for the presenter or the audience. Hearing yourself speak for the first time is unnerving and can add an element of doubt or in confidence in your speech.

You'll also find clarity an issue on some public address systems. Quite often a hired DJ at a wedding will allow use of the radio mic for speeches. This is a generous gift, although the balance of sound in the equipment may lend more to loud introductions to hit singles than a verbal array of clear words.

Microphones in the main come in four types, the hand-held, lapel, desk or head-set varieties.

The handheld microphone, either wireless or wired is the conventional method of amplification. These devices are not omnidirectional, they do not accept sound from all directions even though the head of the microphone is often shaped like a ball.   A mono-directional microphone helps to stop the device from causing feedback, a high pitched whistle caused by the vocal leaving the speakers and being caught in a loop with the microphone itself. From a user's point of view, the mono-directional microphone means that you need to speak directly into the top of the device for it to operate correctly. It often feels more comfortable to hold the base end to your chest whilst talking at a slight angle to microphone itself. This can often cause intermittent pick up and dropout. You can very quickly create the downward spiral of misunderstanding, scepticism and boredom if the sound is not continuous and clear.

The lapel microphone is a favourite on speaking tours and corporate presentations. The microphone itself is housed in a small clip that attaches to clothing approximately 8 inches below the mouth. These are generally wireless devices and the radio unit is attached to a belt or waistline, hidden beneath a jacket or jumper. There are two things to be aware of. The first is that the cable should be hidden beneath your clothes so that it cannot be snagged or caught whilst the person is speaking. This would have the adverse effect of pulling the microphone off or away from the mouth. The second point is that if the microphone is located on one lapel and the head is turned to the opposite side whilst speaking, sound may be lost. This often happens when you turn around and point at the PowerPoint slide.

The head-set microphone is now becoming the most popular and reliable method of capturing the sound in a performance. A microphone placed directly beside your mouth in this way will not fluctuate even during movement. It is often a good idea with the slimmer versions of these devices to secure them to the face and trailing wires to the neck with flesh coloured tape. This is an added safety feature which cannot be detected whilst sitting inside the audience.

The use of laptops
In some circumstances a laptop or tablet is an ideal medium for delivering information or offering proof of concept to the audience. This may be on a one-to-one

basis or to a wider audience using Microsoft PowerPoint and a digital projector.

Let's take a small presentation first of all. Perhaps you have a software app or web site you are trying to promote and the audience are two people sat at a table in a coffee shop. It is natural to sit opposite someone while you speak to them. Making eye contact shows sincerity and as we have already discussed you need to look at the audience to see their reaction to your information.

The problem with a laptop in close quarters is that the screen and keyboard are only located on the side of the user. So, at some point the machine needs to be manipulated and then rotated so that the audience can see what is going on.

A poor presenter will often keep the lion's share of the screen in their eye line making it easy for them to operate. In this case the audience have to strain their vision or lean to one side to get a better view. This is not ideal. The customer is king, remember that. Your laptop needs to be positioned directly in front of them so they have the best view possible. It is so easy for an audience to give up on an item before they've seen it, simply because the effort needed creates demotivation, not curiosity.

Make sure that you know the software so well that you can operate it, upside down and back to front without looking. Know where the buttons are and what keyboard short cuts will make your life easier. Instead of using the track pad, consider adding a USB mouse so that you can operate the device to the side of the audience. In this scenario, one of the best ways to gain complete attention, is to let the audience use the mouse and keyboard on your instruction.

In a larger presentation using PowerPoint you generally find two set ups. The first is where the audience is sat in a theatre style with the presenter standing next to the projection screen and the second is where the audience is sat around a board room style table. Both examples offer their own challenges.

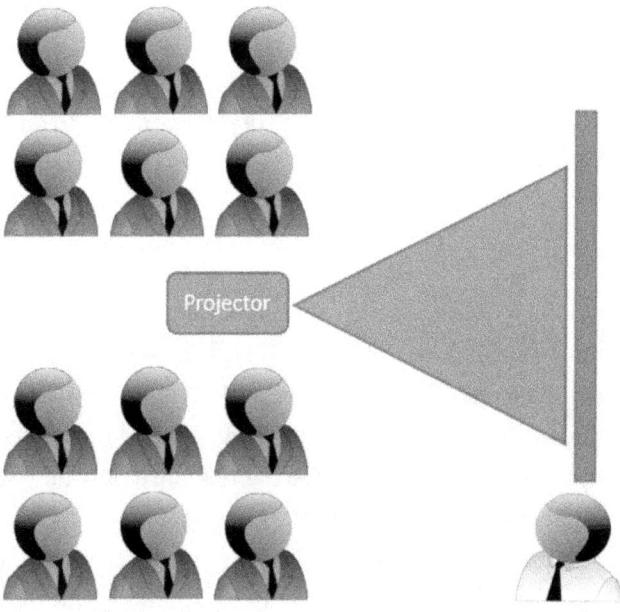

(Theatre Style - This is an ideal set-up, the audience can see the screen and the presenter can see the audience.)

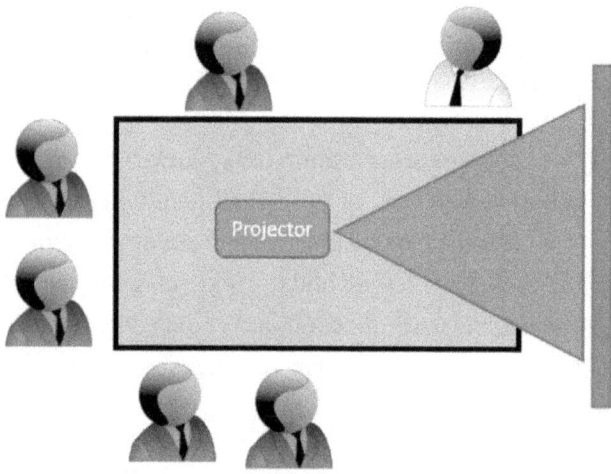

(Boardroom Presentation – this may be a flat screen TV or projector onto a wall, the presenter needs to look at the audience.)

Sometimes the projector cable is so short that the presenter sits directly behind or to the side projector looking in exactly the same direction as the audience. This is a mistake. The number one rule is to look at the audience and to observe your effect on them. Remember, the meaning of the communication is the response that you get. If you cannot see the response how do you know that the presentation is effective and if it isn't effective, how will you change your style so that it is? Buy a longer projector cable, it isn't expensive and tape it to the floor so that no one trips over it.

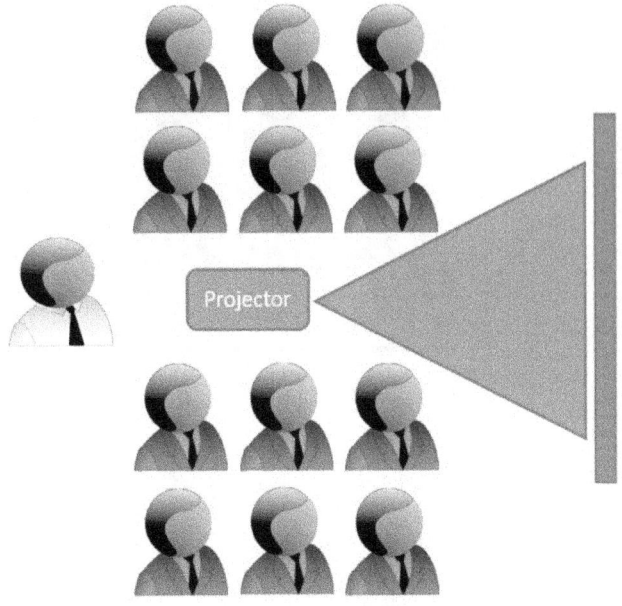

(Theatre Style – by sitting behind the audience this presenter is losing eye contact. When this presenter makes an important point the audience may turn around to acknowledge the fact and by the end of the performance suffer a stiff neck.)

I said a moment ago, know your PowerPoint slides and software so well that you can operate it with your head up 99% of the time, or you will miss those communication gems. There is no need for you to turn round and look at the projector screen because you have a screen directly in front of you.

(Boardroom Presentation – Angle your laptop so that you are facing the audience.)

If you sit beside the projector, you create presenter tennis. This is a fun activity for both parties, the presenter and audience. You announce the slide, the audience looks up and reads the information from the screen, then you make an important point vocally and they look back at you and so on. I am being facetious. Presenter tennis soon becomes annoying. You end up with the looking only at the screen and ignoring the presenter.

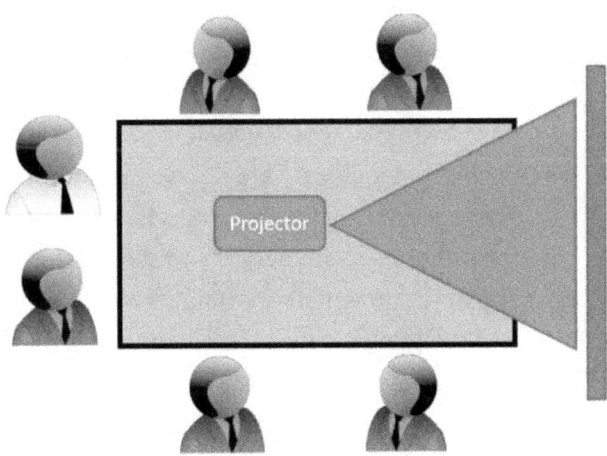

(Presenter Tennis – avoid at all costs.)

If you are presenting with PowerPoint and the laptop is in front of you make the movement of the slides easy. Use the down arrow to move forward and up arrow to move backwards. The mouse and fancy clicker devices, so often fail. You could of course, ask someone else to do it for you, but ensure they practice your presentation with you a few times to make the changes slick. Strangely enough, you don't need to stop talking between slides, a slick presentation will continue with the slides in a supporting role.

If you are showing software or web applications remember these golden rules.

- The audience have never seen this product before and will take a while to get used to the interface. Slow down, explain what's familiar in the interface, how it works and how easy it is.
- Things that look easy are always more appealing. There are of course, exceptions to that rule. Computer programmers like to see behind the scenes, but the mere mortals among us won't buy into the thing if it looks too hard to use.
- Moving the mouse quickly just creates confusion. Try moving the cursor to a button of importance, circle the button and explain what it does. This focuses the audience's eye, they will listen to your words. Then pause before explaining the next feature. Good practise is to let go of the mouse and continue speaking.

The lectern and other obstacles

Lecterns can be useful items to rest notes and computers on during the presentation. They can also be an obstacle to the audience who are trying to see the real you. By standing behind a lectern you may lose that sense of connection. Be aware of your choices before you attend. Sometimes the public address system is fed from two pencil style microphones on the lectern and therefore the speaker cannot leave that area and still be heard.

An optional lapel microphone may offer the freedom to move nearer to your audience. With the style of preparation you have been taught in this book, you will have the confidence to leave the relative safety of the lectern.   The confidence you now hold from practising your presentation out loud means that movement can be an added feature of your performance.

Move freely, but avoid standing in front of the screen. Make sure everyone in the room can see your presentation.

Section 3 - Perform

In the first two sections of this book, prepare and practice, you learned how to design a masterful presentation and how to deliver it in a congruent fashion. All things equal, these two topics alone will have made you more than competent presenter. So, it is important now to relax. Stop the stress and realise how prepared you already are to get on that stage and be a master presenter.

In the final section, perform we are going to fine tune your ability to make change. Remember you have an objective to achieve in the presentation. This objective is to convince the audience of something. Maybe the topic of the presentation is computer hardware and your objective is to convince new customers to take up your offers. Or you are a hairdresser at a business breakfast meeting and you have fifteen minutes to rally new custom. Or the parent of a child that has received lifesaving treatment at a hospital and you want to advertise their good work and motivate donations. These are clear objectives.

For these objectives to succeed you need the audience to make an emotional shift. Change in people only takes place when emotions are created and discharged. The urge to buy the latest laptop or pair of shoes or gadget is an emotion inside you. Your life doesn't depend on the purchase, it isn't life or death it is an urge to do so, an emotion.

Even when you present a concrete return on investment case to a managing director, the outcome is motivated by how the person feels about you, your business and your proposition. The unconscious mind is building a picture of the presenter right from the start. Are they dressed correctly? Do I feel they are truthful? Is this the right deal for me and my company? Do I think I can do business with this person?

Building emotions

Consider climbing a mountain for a moment. At the bottom you are full of energy and excited, up beat in fact. Then the work begins, easy at first. The foothills are a stretch of the limbs and the weather is calm. The climb makes you dig deep, using muscles you never knew you had. Then the summit and euphoria. You've done it, you've shared the achievement with friends and claim proud bragging rights.

Isn't this a presentation, in terms of emotion?

It would be hard, but not impossible to start a presentation from a negative emotion.

"I've come here today to talk about the dying in Africa."

I agree this speech should have negative emotion involved, but not at the start.

Exactly as if you are climbing a mountain, start on a positive high. Explain what you are going to tell them. What are they going to get out of their time with you? What's in it for them?

Next, change the mood, as you climb the foot hills. We only need a slight change of emotional value at this point, not a massive one. Don't go from laughter to tears in one go or it won't look sincere. Perhaps you reduce the brightness of your voice, insert a little silence here and there and change your demeanour on stage. You are warning the subconscious minds of the audience that change is afoot.

Now, go for the big one. Tell a true story. It's a good idea to have two associations that the audience can make. Go for the sad association first and then a happy one, two emotions in one story. An abbreviated version of the story could be.

"On my first visit to Africa in 2010 over 10,000 men, women and children lost their lives, I can't tell you how heart breaking this was to see. (Pause and begin the build-up) I am pleased to say with the money raised at these events has made an important difference (now up beat and hopeful)"

Or perhaps you are motivating staff at an engineering plant.

"You may have been aware of the commitment of the office staff and management team in recent months to hold onto existing clients to secure all of our futures. I can reveal that without their deliberate hard work, the survival of this business may have taken a different turn. (Pause and build) I truly believe, the bad times are behind us now. The manufacturing and engineering elements have always been an outstanding part of what we do, thanks to you. We now have a clear and bright future as along as we stay focussed."

You have to be honest with yourself and the audience or your emotions won't look sincere. This is the most powerful technique you have in your arsenal, use it wisely and always practice.

The hypnotic effect
The eminent master hypnotist Igor Ledochowski teaches his clients that you need to achieve three elements before the audience will accept your suggestions, this is called the ABS formula.

Attention – Before you start to deliver information, you need to gain the full attention of who you are speaking to. If there is a distraction in the room, someone talking or music in the distance or whispering at the back, you stand the high risk of failure. Resolve the issue first, you have the power to do this. If someone is speaking, make a joke of it, 'can I join in' or say to the others 'I need everyone's attention before I go on'. The pressure from the other audience members will resolve this situation.

Bypass critical thinking – If you make a sales pitch, the majority of the audience will realise what you are doing and not get enthusiastic about your words and their meanings. Help the audience to relax at first. Don't put pressure on the audience at the start telling them that you would like a donation or that you want them to buy.   Fill them with confidence. Talk about how you are the specialist or the expert in this topic. Even if you aren't, 'fake it to make it'. Be positive about your association with the topic.

"Companies that have used this product always recommend it to other people."

The word always does not have a cotton wool meaning. Change the word always for sometimes and you will not achieve your desired result.

Stimulate the unconscious mind – Allow the audience to see the possibilities of your solution. As they are paying attention to you in a relaxed state, the words that you deliver will penetrate deep inside the unconscious mind. Accentuate these words with emotion and change will happen. You will move your audience from a state of abject apathy to a call to action. A motivation that you will physically see. So much so that after your performance, more and more people will congratulate you on.

By installing this belief in your own subconscious awareness you become a master presenter that can affect the minds over everyone you meet, in exactly the same way a hypnotist controls the stage.

Another technique that hypnotists use is to anchor a theme or idea. Anchors are abundant in society and they ignite emotion which is one of the key drivers in our presentations. Say for example that you take a walk along the sea front and you smell candy floss and you smile. What is it about the smell of candy floss that changes your emotion? The reason is that earlier in your life you have made an association with that smell at a good time in your life. Maybe as a child you had a party and the candy floss was there.

Negative anchors also exist. Perhaps a piece of music reminds you of a relative that has passed away or you see a pet your departed friend owned, which reignites the distress you felt at the funeral.   Anchors may last forever. So, if you are wanting to make a point that you want everyone to remember, link every topic and theme to that anchor.   Show the audience the associations and allow these to develop. You are creating a long lasting memory.

In PowerPoint you could build an image, one piece at a time that represents your message. Let's take the example that your speech is about speed improvements in deliveries that you company has invested in.   The picture could be the components of a sports car, the engine (your employees), the body work (head office), the speedometer (the measurement of speed increase) and tyres (continued stability). By adding elements of the picture at each section of your speech, the audience will be using their visual representation system to imagine them using the service in their minds eye.

Repetition is also a favourite in the hypnotist's arsenal. There is no point saying someone once and expecting your audience to act on the information. In exactly the same way that you learn, repeat the punch line over and over. You don't have to say the important bits in the same way every time, mix up your method. Consider using all of the senses, sight, sound, feel, smells and tastes.

Get the audience involved
All the way through this book I have talked about the importance of emotion to cement your ideas in the minds of the audience.   This is not the only way to motivate them.   When you are in the audience you sit still. More often than not you only use your sensory perception to pick up what the speaker is saying. Sight, sound, smell, all pay their part.

What would happen if you got your audience to move or speak?

To the new and uninitiated speaker the words, audience participation may fill them with fear, but here's the thing. The more a person is involved in the interaction, the easier it is for them to accept the change. If someone sits in front of you and doesn't say anything, how do you know they are in agreement? Reading body language is a wonderful art, but can you do this with a room of people successfully, probably not.

A few years ago, there seemed to be endless sales people selling watches in the car par park of the local services. Every time you left your car to go to the shop or restaurant you would be approached by an individual with the deal of a life time.   Now I don't condone or like the antics of these people, but one successful technique used by them did catch my eye. The moment they found a person interested they would hand them the watch and the sales person would put their hands in their pockets. You see, the moment you hold something, an emotion called desire takes over. A few words of encouragement and the audience are more likely to buy, plus of course, the audience cannot leave as the sales person keeps his hands in his pocket.

The same thing can be translated into any seminar or presentation situation. The moment that you have gained interest, why not hand the item you are discussing over to the audience to allow the emotion to build. This desire is the emotion that will make the sale. Let's say for instance, that you are selling computer software. It is all well and good that the customer sees you demonstrating the product, but it is even more powerful when they can do this themselves.

If you are selling software then make sure that you pick a simple routine that the customer can easily follow so that they don't become confused. Confusion is an emotion that can easily stop the sale going ahead. Let's take the scenario of cookery lessons. You may be doing a demonstration to promote a new cookery course to passers-by at an exhibition. Allowing the passers-by to touch the dough, to touch the machinery and smell the bread cooking means that your audience is involved and is more likely to buy in to your message.

Another area to consider with audiences is participation with asking questions. One of the problems with questions is that they can easily disturb the flow of the information from the speaker. You may be just getting into your stride and a question might undermine the information that you are giving. Although this might be a negative side-effect, in the main questions are a good thing that allow you to express your knowledge of the subject. What we do need to do is consider the timing of the presentation and ensure that we do not overrun where possible.

At the start of your presentation when you begin to set the objectives, you may want to indicate that there is an appropriate time to ask questions. This might be at the end of the presentation or at predetermined times in the middle. By setting the format of the presentation, the topics and the objectives at the start, you can set the scene appropriately. For instance, no one will ask about price if you have told them that all of this detail will be covered after the demonstration.

First of all let's examine the reasons why questions occur. Sometimes the audience is very eager to learn and even though you have created a well laid plan of information some audience members want to jump the gun and find out the detail first. The detail being requested might be of course be price. It may not be a good idea to let this piece of information out into the domain of the audience until they have been able to see the benefit of the solution that you are offering. You might answer with:

"That's a very good question and I'm glad you brought that up. In a moment I am going give you a full breakdown of the pricing to ensure that you have everything before you leave."

Questions are often asked if the audience is either sceptical or have misunderstood and element of the presentation. You'll hear something like:

"I'm not sure that this product can do what you're saying it will do."

This is a sceptical response. Or you may hear a phrase like "how do you expect my company to buy this product if it doesn't have European approval?" (In this particular case, you do have European approval), this response comes from the audience misunderstanding your message.

In both cases and more often than not, this is the fault of the presenter and the way that the information is being delivered. It isn't a problem and can actually be a benefit in the presentation. The reason being is that others in the audience will be thinking the same thing. To resolve these issues you must follow this procedure.

- Understand the issue
- Empathise with the person
- Offer proof
- Ask for acceptance

It is often the case that the question being asked differs in some way, to the answer that you want to give. It is also for the benefit of the audience that you ask for clarity before you proceed. This shows that you have empathy with the situation in the first place. Take a look at this question from an audience member.

"Can I ask, when will the product have European approval?"

"I'll be happy to answer that question, would you mind me asking is European approval important in your particular business?"

"Yes it is, European approval is becoming a hot topic and everything that I purchase needs to conform, so that I can keep my status as a preferred supplier."

"I am pleased to say that our product is fully accredited in this area, I'm really glad you brought that up. If you take a look at the back of the brochure in the packs on your seats, you'll see the European symbol of excellence. We also believe as a company, that this is the most important way forward."

"Does that answer your question?"

The short response to something that looks pretty minor, might actually be something that is really important to this business. It may have been something that has caused a great deal of pain and anguish to the person in the audience. You really aren't going to know that until you ask them a question. It doesn't matter how insignificant the question may be or how complex, all questions should be answered with the same level of empathy.

The reason you do this, is that you are training the audience with your professionalism on the easier and less significant questions. However, when a more significant and complex question comes along it looks to the audience that you are in control of the situation. You've given your answer a lot of thought and sincerity.

It is important to ask for acceptance at the end of your answer. Never leave the question open even if you find it's a question that you cannot answer. If you cannot answer the question for whatever reason be honest. You may say "that's a really good question and one for our technical person to answer at the end. I'll ask him to join us in a moment so that you can leave with all the information, is that okay?"

There are times as well when the audience can get too comfortable. Especially if the presentations have gone on for a long time. I saw a recent seminar which was hosted by an ex-paratrooper. In the morning it was very entertaining, he interjected stories about the army with the serious subject that we were there to discuss. The morning was intermingled with other speakers, also with interesting topics, but there were hours between coffee breaks. In the afternoon, the dead zone arrived.

The dead zone is the time directly after lunch, when most people have eaten and their attention span is at an all-time low. On this particular day the paratrooper came out on stage wearing PT kit. It appears that part of his military training was to exercise the troops. He spent the next fifteen minutes getting the audience to move, by jumping up and down by following high paced military commands. It was all done in a spirit of good fun. The audience loved it and by the end were all high and motivated.

Not everybody has the ability and the confidence to get people out of their seats like an entertainer would. There is nothing stopping you though from building into your presentation a task of movement. Perhaps you may have taped an envelope to the underside of the chair with a prize in it. Everybody has to move their chair to look for the prize or you ask the audience to move to a different part of the room and introduce themselves to new people. Any sort of movement will be appreciated if the presentation is going to go on for a while.

I mentioned a moment ago about putting packs of information on the chairs of the people that you are speaking to. Packs of information are useful for the attendee, but issued at the wrong time can prove a distraction. Let's say for example, you are sitting in a boardroom and in front of each delegate you hand them a pack of brochures, a writing pad, a pen, etc

On the face of it, this looks like a good thing to do. At the end of the day you want the person to leave with a price list and brochure and something to remember you by. The problem you have is, the audience may sit and read the brochures while you are speaking. This is not a good thing. Remember attention is what you need to make a successful presentation.

Perhaps, you put in front of each delegate a pen and a pad of paper so that they can make notes. At the end of the presentation, you say that "the information I promised you is in packs at the back of the room. What I need you to do is fill out the feedback form and my colleagues will let you have those before you leave." And the benefit now is, that the audience can make notes while you're speaking. Notes that mean something to them. You have promised them prices and of course, they will get them, but they have to do some work first filling out the feedback form. This also ensures that you capture their entire information for marketing purposes before they leave.

End effectively

The final tip I can give you in this section is the importance of ending effectively. If you have spoken for forty minutes, you may find that you have begun to run out of steam. The same can be said of your audience in fact, after thirty minutes or so, the audience need to be woken up.

I appreciate that I have said, tell the audience exactly what time the presentation is going to finish and do not overrun. With all of the practice that you've put in, you will finish on time. Build to a crescendo, a positive message with a strong call to action. The call to action is what you have set out to achieve. This is your objective.

There is nothing stopping you from generating an atmosphere at the end. By ending on a strong statement and starting a round of applause, you will enable the audience to tell you that they have enjoyed the whole event. You may like to prompt them and say that you will be around afterwards to answer any more questions or leave them your email address.

The art of being a master presenter is being willing to try new things and cross boundaries. The Hypnotic Wisdom of Presentation Mastery contains all the tools you need to be a success. Whether you're new to presenting or a professional wanting to get better, take each section in your stride and practice, practice, practice.

Appendix – Adjustments for certain situations

The best man speech

For most of us being a best man is a once-in-a-lifetime opportunity. Most of us want to do the best job we can and enjoy the experience. The first thing to do is always get a heads up on the wedding itself. The bride and groom will always have a specific picture in mind of the type of event and speeches that they want.

It is important that you respect their wishes. Listen carefully and even make notes because it is going to be impossible to give this speech to them before the event. Understand the etiquette of the day, whether the wedding is a formal or informal affair, it is easy for you then to fit in your ideas.

Preparation is everything. Get the preparation phase of the speech out of the way as early as possible. You may know that this wedding is going to take place in six months' time. It is better to have the preparation done immediately than wait till the last minute. At the end of the day, once the speech is prepared it can be altered to allow for new facts as they arise. Early preparation means that you have the chance to run through the speech many times before the day.

You may find that you can become so confident that you can add jokes or comedy in certain areas. As this is the more complex area of presentations it is far better to try the jokes out with a friend in real life before including them. At the end of the day, enjoy yourself. When you have your speech down and prepared to a high standard, you will really enjoy the day and be part of the wedding. If you are not prepared, the day can seem very daunting and not a day you will want to remember.

The comedic champion

I am in awe of comedians. I find it very hard to sit and watch a comedian and not critique the presentation style. If this is something you really want to do, then seek advice from other comedians on the subject of telling jokes and writing material. You may still use the same techniques to do with collating the information and practising.

Practising out loud, over and over can never be a bad thing. Use a video camera to get the best results. Seeing yourself in action, I'm sure will give you the confidence to make changes. A comedian like every presenter has to stand in the wings waiting for his turn. By being prepared you will reduce the amount of anticipation and relax. A relaxed performance is what the audience is looking for.

Demonstrating a product

When you are selling a product make sure that you are committed and enthusiastic about the thing that you are selling. If you aren't 100% convinced by the product you are selling your congruency will show to the audience. Be knowledgeable, know more about your product than your competitors. Aim to be a trusted adviser, an expert, a specialist. Buyers always want to purchase from people that know what they're doing and may even pay a little bit more for an experts services.

Keep it simple. Whatever you say about the product, make sure that everyone, including someone that knows nothing about what you're talking about, can come on board and use it. The easier it is, the easier it will be to sell. If possible, allow your customers or prospects to play with the item. Let them touch it, let them feel it or let them smell it. Use all of a person's perceptive senses to add to the experience.

Presenting one-on-one to a colleague
Now that you have all the skills of a master presenter it would be easy to overlook the people that are nearest to you, such as colleagues or close friends. These people already expect you to be a poor presenter. This is not the case and you need to show them exactly how professional you can be.

If you let them drive the meeting you can, but this is a poor way to present. They may want to ask lots of questions and forego the formality of the presentation. Don't allow them to do this. It won't take long for you to increase your standing in the business with your new found skills. What may once have been offered to another member of staff will now be offered to you.

A performance hypnotist

I am a performance hypnotist and I can say that learning the art of stage hypnosis is as much to do with the many years of presentation skills that I have learned as it is hypnosis. A performance hypnotist, stage hypnotist or street hypnotist as they like to be called are simply presenters that have learned the art of communication.

You may believe that when you see a hypnotist in action that the words they use are developed for each situation. An ad lib cacophony that deals with each new person and request. This is simply not the case. The hypnotist learns his words off rote, which means that they are the same words and phrases for every performance. They are simply delivered as if they have never been said before.

What I mean is, as a performer I give the impression that this is new routine every single time that I do it. Even if people have seen me before the way that the words are delivered makes people think that this is a new performance and it is simply a technique.

Hypnosis is simply an art form of communication skills and for those of you that want to learn more, there is an abundant amount of material on the Internet and I am happy to answer any questions you may have.

Motivating players on a sports field

There are so many good sports films that have been made that show the captain or the coach delivering impassioned speeches to the players in the dressing room. This is a good place to start. Watch the films and see the passion. Passion is always used to motivate. Understand what it is that motivates your team.

Ensure that when you speak to the players you alternate between working as a team and the importance of individuals and their roles in success. Make sure that everybody leaves the dressing room with no doubt what their role is. Make sure that no one is left out or feels demotivated by the words that you say.